Gaius Valerius Catullus, James Cranstoun

The Poems of Valerius Catullus

With life of the poet, excursûs, and illustrative notes

Gaius Valerius Catullus, James Cranstoun

The Poems of Valerius Catullus
With life of the poet, excursûs, and illustrative notes

ISBN/EAN: 9783337006181

Printed in Europe, USA, Canada, Australia, Japan

Cover: Foto ©Thomas Meinert / pixelio.de

More available books at **www.hansebooks.com**

THE POEMS

OF

VALERIUS CATULLUS,

TRANSLATED INTO ENGLISH VERSE.

WITH

LIFE OF THE POET, EXCURSÛS, AND
ILLUSTRATIVE NOTES.

BY

JAMES CRANSTOUN, B.A.

"—— spirat adhuc amor."

EDINBURGH:
WILLIAM P. NIMMO.
1867.

JOANNI CARMICHAEL, A.M., EDIMB.,

IN SCHOLA REGIA EDIMBURGENSI

MAGISTRO,

VIRO OPTIMO ET ERUDITISSIMO,

PIETATIS CAUSA,

CATULLI VERONENSIS LIBELLUM,

AB SE INTERPRETATUM,

D. D. D.

JACOBUS CRANSTOUN.

PREFACE.

THE following version of the Poems of Catullus—executed during the translator's leisure hours—is submitted to the public, not with the view of superseding existing translations, but of more widely diffusing an acquaintance with a poet who is now beginning to meet with some degree of the attention he deserves. The plan of reproducing all the poems may appear objectionable to some; but to the translator it seemed preferable to that of mutilating the poet, and presenting him in a totally different aspect from that in which he has revealed himself in his writings. Moreover, a translator, if he is anxious to give anything like an exact reflex of his author—which ought surely to be his highest aim—can never be justified in suppressing the one half of his works merely to give him a more respectable appearance. Of all the Latin poets, Catullus, perhaps, can least afford to submit to this excising process. His expressions, it is true, are often intensely sensuous, sometimes even grossly licentious, but to obliterate these and to clothe him in the garb of purity would be to misrepresent him entirely. He would be Atys, not Catullus.

In the present translation, except in very rare instances, no omission, even to the extent of a line, has been made, and this has occurred only when it has been deemed inexpedient to give the English equivalents.

Some of the poems, for obvious reasons, have not been rendered with the same verbal accuracy as others, but in all of them it has been the aim of the translator to preserve, so far as possible, the force and spirit of the original.

The notes and excursûs in the latter part of the volume, and more especially the translations of passages, principally from the Augustan and post-Augustan poets, will, it is hoped, prove interesting to those who are engaged in the actual study of Catullus.

These could easily have been multiplied, and parallels and imitations introduced from modern poets, but they would have swelled the bulk of the volume to an extent never contemplated.

The translator would here gratefully acknowledge his obligations to the notes contained in the admirable edition of "Catullus" by Doering, to the "Roman Poets of the Republic" by Professor Sellar, and to the articles on Latin poetry, by the Rev. Henry Thompson, in the *Encyclopaedia Metropolitana*, as well as to the *Observationes Criticae* (*Catullianae*) of Haupt, the *Quaestiones Catullianae* of Schwabe, and the few but valuable textual remarks of Rossbach, prefixed to his careful edition of Catullus.

To Professor Sellar of the University of Edinburgh, to Professor Nichol of the University of Glasgow, and to his much-esteemed friend Mr John Carmichael of the High School of Edinburgh, the translator's special thanks are due, for much valuable assistance, most cordially given, during the progress of the work.

The text principally followed, although every available one has been consulted, is that of Doering.

When it has been materially departed from, the edition which has been followed is specified.

Should this translation be the means of making the works of Catullus better known, or of affording some slight aid to the youthful student, the translator will consider himself amply repaid for his self-imposed and by no means irksome toil.

GRAMMAR SCHOOL, KIRKCUDBRIGHT,
March 1867.

CONTENTS.

	PAGE
Life of Catullus,	3
I. To Cornelius Nepos,	27
II. To Lesbia's Sparrow,	28
III. On the Death of the Sparrow,	29
IV. Dedication of his Pinnace,	30
V. To Lesbia,	31
VI. To Flavius,	32
VII. To Lesbia,	33
VIII. To Himself, on Lesbia's Inconstancy,	34
IX. To Verannius, on his Return from Spain,	35
X. On the Mistress of Varus,	35
XI. To Furius and Aurelius—the Farewell Message to Lesbia,	37
XII. To Asinius,	38
XIII. To Fabullus—Invitation to Dinner,	39
XIV. To Licinius Calvus,	40
XV. To Aurelius,	41
XVI. To Aurelius and Furius,	42
XVII. To a Certain Town,	43
XVIII. To the Garden God,	45
XIX. The Garden God,	45
XX. The Garden God,	46
XXI. To Aurelius,	47

		PAGE
XXII.	To Varus,	48
XXIII.	To Furius,	49
XXIV.	To a Beauty,	50
XXV.	To Thallus,	50
XXVI.	To Furius,	51
XXVII.	To his Cupbearer—*Two Versions*,	52
XXVIII.	To Verannius and Fabullus,	53
XXIX.	On Mamurra, Addressed to Caesar,	54
XXX.	To Alphenus,	55
XXXI.	To the Peninsula of Sirmio, on his Return to his Villa there,	56
XXXII.	To Ipsithilla,	57
XXXIII.	On the Vibennii,	58
XXXIV.	Hymn to Diana,	59
XXXV.	To Caecilius,	60
XXXVI.	On the Annals of Volusius,	61
XXXVII.	To the Frequenters of a Certain Tavern,	62
XXXVIII.	To Cornificius,	63
XXXIX.	On Egnatius,	64
XL.	To Ravidus,	65
XLI.	On the Mistress of Formianus,	65
XLII.	On a Certain Female,	66
XLIII.	On the Mistress of Formianus,	67
XLIV.	To his Farm,	67
XLV.	On Acme and Septimius,	68
XLVI.	To Himself, on the Return of Spring,	70
XLVII.	To Porcius and Socration,	70
XLVIII.	On a Beauty,	71
XLIX.	To Cicero,	71
L.	To Licinius,	72
LI.[a]	To Lesbia,	73
LI.[b]	Fragment,	74
LII.	To Himself, on Struma and Vatinius,	74
LIII.	On Somebody and Calvus,	74
LIV.	To Caesar,	75
LV.	To Camerius,	75

		PAGE
LVI.	To Cato,	77
LVII.	To Mamurra and Caesar,	77
LVIII.	To Coelius, Concerning Lesbia,	78
LIX.	On Rufa and Rufulus,	78
LX.	Fragment,	79
LXI.	Nuptial Song in Honour of Junia and Manlius,	79
LXII.	Nuptial Song,	89
LXIII.	Atys,	94
LXIV.	The Nuptials of Peleus and Thetis,	101
LXV.	To Hortalus,	130
LXVI.	Beronice's Hair,	131
LXVII.	Dialogue between Catullus and a Door,	135
LXVIII.ᵃ	Epistle to Manlius,	137
LXVIII.ᵇ	To Allius,	139
LXIX.	To Rufus,	145
✓ LXX.	On the Inconstancy of Woman's Love,	145
LXXI.	To Virro,	146
LXXII.	To Lesbia,	146
LXXIII.	On an Ingrate,	147
LXXIV.	On Gellius,	148
LXXV.	To Lesbia,	148
LXXVI.	To Himself.—The Lover's Petition,	149
LXXVII.	To Rufus,	150
LXXVIII.	On Gallus,	151
LXXIX.	On Lesbius,	152
LXXX.	To Gellius,	152
LXXXI.	To a Beauty,	153
LXXXII.	To Quintius,	154
LXXXIII.	On the Husband of Lesbia,	154
LXXXIV.	On Arrius,	155
LXXXV.	On his Love—*Two Versions*,	155, 156
LXXXVI.	Quintia and Lesbia Compared,	156
LXXXVII.	To Lesbia (translated in LXXV.),	157
LXXXVIII.	On Gellius,	157
LXXXIX.	On Gellius,	157

		PAGE
XC.	On Gellius,	158
XCI.	On Gellius,	158
XCII.	On Lesbia,	159
XCIII.	On Caesar,	159
XCIV.	On Mamurra,	160
XCV.	On "Smyrna," a Poem by Cinna,	160
XCVI.	To Calvus, on the Death of Quintilia,	161
XCVII.	On Aemilius,	161
XCVIII.	To Vettius,	162
XCIX.	The Kiss.—To a Beauty,	163
C.	On Coelius and Quintius,	164
CI.	The Poet at his Brother's Grave—*Two Versions*,	165
CII.	To Cornelius,	166
CIII.	To Silo,	167
CIV.	On Lesbia,	167
CV.	On Mamurra,	167
CVI.	On an Auctioneer and a Pretty Girl,	168
CVII.	To Lesbia.—The Reconciliation,	168
CVIII.	On Cominius,	169
CIX.	To Lesbia,	169
CX.	To Aufilena,	170
CXI.	To Aufilena,	171
CXII.	To Naso,	171
CXIII.	To Cinna,	171
CXIV.	On Mamurra,	172
CXV.	On Mamurra,	172
CXVI.	To Gellius,	173
EXCURSUS AND ILLUSTRATIVE NOTES,		177

CATULLUS.

LIFE OF CATULLUS.

OME, during the first five centuries of her existence, had nothing worthy of the name of a poetical literature. The fanciful theory propounded by Perizonius, and energetically and plausibly defended by Niebuhr, Macaulay, and others, receives no support from the relics of antiquity. Rome had, doubtless, a rich legendary history, but it was mainly traditional; and her records probably owe more of their charm to the imaginative genius of Livy than to the ballads and poetic essays of early bards. The ritual hymns, Fescennine lays, Saturae, festal and funeral songs, which constituted the autochthonous literature of the country, were rude compositions in primitive and inartistic metres, and destitute alike of imagination and poetic fire. They even failed to excite any admiration in the cultivated minds of immediately succeeding generations.

Ennius has written the character of his countrymen in a single line—

"Bellipotentes sunt magi' quam sapientipotentes."

They were essentially a people of arms, not of arts; yet their warlike power was ultimately the means of bringing them under the refining influences of the literature inherited or possessed by the conquered nations. The war with Pyrrhus, and the long siege of Tarentum, were the immediate causes that led to this great change in the national character.

But the subtle genius of the Greek had long been insinuating itself into the southern states of Italy, and from these parts come the first writers who command our attention. These writers stood in the position of aliens to Rome, and owed their culture not to her, but to Magna Graecia. They imbibed the philosophy of Greece; they accepted her theogony; they developed a closely imitative literature—a literature that even among themselves was judged by the Grecian standard, and esteemed in proportion to the accuracy and taste with which the writer reproduced the graces of the Grecian mind. To this period belong the names of Livius Andronicus, Naevius, Ennius, Plautus, Caecilius, Terence, Pacuvius, Attius, and Lucilius. Livius Andronicus was a

Greek, and deserves notice here more from his having been the medium through which the Romans first became acquainted, in their own tongue, with the works of his countrymen, than from any original power or merits of his own.

Naevius, in his epic poem on the first Punic war, was the last of the Roman poets who employed the old Saturnian or native measure.

Ennius produced an epic, Greek in type, but Roman in subject and spirit, that furnished matter for reproduction and imitation to all who afterwards essayed the same task. But, apart from their indebtedness to Greek literature, these last two were men of vigorous mind, and are in every way entitled to rank as great poets. Plautus, Caecilius, Terence, Pacuvius, and Attius—all born outside the boundaries of Latium, and deriving from foreign influences their culture and knowledge of the poetic art, were mainly employed in adapting to the Roman stage the works of the Greek dramatists.

Lucilius alone was a Latin by birth; but he was in an equal degree indebted to Greek literature. He has, however, the high merit of developing a distinct species of poetry. Formal satire had hitherto been unknown both to the Greeks and Romans. Among the former, satire had been confined to the comic drama; indeed, among a people like the Greeks, of fine sensibilities, whose ideal of life naturally sought visible representation in dramatic display, comedy would seem to have been the proper form of satiric composition. Among the latter, it sprung up in the primitive scenic medley, and partook more of the nature of low buffoonery and coarse scurrility than of the wit, verve, and caustic humour of the brilliant Attic comedy. It was next adapted to the Roman taste in the pieces which the above-mentioned writers had borrowed from Greek originals. But with the blunt, straightforward, matter of-fact Roman—the man of practicality, *par excellence*,—satire, in order to its complete development and intelligent appreciation, required to take the form of a direct empiric philosophy. It did so with Lucilius, and what was the consequence? Unlike the borrowed forms of literature, it had a vigorous youth, a vigorous manhood a vigorous age. The genius of comedy disappeared with Plautus, Terence, and Attius, and the productions of these writers were soon forced to give place to the beast-fights and man-fights of the amphitheatre and the games of the circus. The Epic of Ennius and the Epic of Virgil—themselves inferior to their model—were succeeded by feebler efforts. The original and profound speculations of Plato and Aristotle awoke no deeper echo in the Roman mind than the fine oratorical treatises of Cicero. Catullus and Horace were the only poets who worthily struck the Æolian lyre. It was different in the case of Satire. This native product of Roman genius, strong, keen, Roman-like in Lucilius, attained unequalled perfection in Horace, and, as if catching fresh fire from the hell of Roman depravity, reappeared long afterwards with unabated power and the despairing earnestness of righteous ire in the great satirist of the empire.

After Lucilius, nearly half a century elapsed before another luminary appeared in the poetical horizon. The language, however, was becoming gradually moulded for the purposes of the artist; conquered Greece had yielded up the poetry and philosophy of ages as an everlasting heritage to her barbarian conquerors; the Grecising tendency of past generations was still on the increase, when two poets of rare genius appeared: Titus Lucretius Carus, the author of the noblest didactic poem of ancient or modern times, and Q. or C. Valerius Catullus.[1]

According to the Eusebian Chronicle, Catullus

---

[1] He is called Quintus by Pliny the Elder, (*Nat. Hist.* xxxvii. cap. 6,) and Caius by Appuleius, (in *Apologia*.) If reliance could be placed on Jos. Scaliger's reading of a very corrupt line, (Carm. lxvii. 12,) which he testifies to finding clearly written on the copy of James Cujas or Cujacius, a French jurist of the sixteenth century, Quintus is undoubtedly his prænomen.

Scaliger's reading of the line is—
"Verum istis populi naenia, Quinte, facit."
Lachmann conjectures—
"Verum istud populi fabula, Quinte, facit."
We leave it to the reader to set what value he pleases on the readings of these two scholars.

was born B.C. 87, in the consulship of Cneius Octavius and Lucius Cornelius Cinna, and died at the age of thirty, B.C. 57. The latter date is clearly incorrect, as one of his poems[1] plainly testifies that he was alive in the consulship of Vatinius, B.C. 47. This fact is enough to throw doubt on the date there assigned to his birth, and, indeed, when all the circumstances are considered, we are led to the conclusion that the error in the one case is as great as in the other.[2]

The mistake of the chronicler may have arisen from the name of the consul, for it is extremely probable that he was born in the consulship of another Cneius Octavius, who held office with Marcus Scribonius Curio B.C. 76. Assuming this to be the case, there is no difficulty in believing that he died at the age of thirty, as there is nothing in his writings to show that he was living after B.C. 46.

Catullus was born at Verona,[3] or in its immediate vicinity. Whether he belonged to a branch of the illustrious family of the Valerii it is impossible to say; but it is evident that his father must have been a person

---

[1] lii.

[2] *Many* of the poems of Catullus were clearly written after B.C. 56, while only *one* can with certainty be dated before that year, viz., the 46th, which appears to have been written in B.C. 57.

[3] lxvii. 34. Ov. Amor. iii., *El.* xv. 7. Mart. i. 62; x. 103; xiv 195.

of considerable position, as we learn from Suetonius[1] that he was the friend and frequent entertainer of Julius Caesar. He probably remained in his native place till he assumed the *toga virilis*, which we cannot far err in supposing he did about the age of fifteen or sixteen. He then went to Rome, where, in all likelihood, for two years he led a gay and extravagant life.[2] His expenditure at this time would seem to have equalled, perhaps even exceeded, his income, if we are to put anything like a literal construction on his occasional outcries against poverty.[3] This we can hardly do, for about this time, or very shortly after it, a splendid villa at Sirmio,[4] if not, indeed, the whole peninsula, either by inheritance or by purchase, came into his possession. On the other hand, it must be admitted that such a banker as Silo,[5] and companions like Furius and Aurelius[6]—if they were really among the poet's acquaintances at this time —must have drawn heavily on even great resources. Whether on account of the unsatisfactory state of his finances, or from the desire to amass a fortune, he set out with a number of especial friends for Bithynia, in the suite of Memmius,[7] B.C. 58. The expedition, however, proved a complete failure, and tired of the service, and disgusted with the meanness

---

[1] Suet. in *Julio*, cap. 73.
[2] Cf. lxviii. 16–18.
[3] *Vide* xiii., xxvi., &c.
[4] xxxi. [5] ciii.
[6] xxi.
[7] x. and xxviii.

and rapacity of his chief, he bade Bithynia and his companions farewell, and set out to visit the great Asiatic cities.[1] After completing his tour in the East he would seem to have had a yacht built expressly for himself at Amastris,[2] on the shores of the Euxine. In it he sailed to Italy, and up the Padus and its tributary, "the smooth-sliding Mincius," till he reached Lake Benacus, (Lago di Garda,) on the bosom of whose waters lay his villa and estate.[3] He probably returned to Italy in B.C. 56, and had certainly settled down in Rome before the impeachment of Vatinius by Calvus, (B.C. 54,) for he tells us that he was present on the occasion, and in a short epigrammatic effusion he pays a humorous tribute to the talents of that distinguished orator.[4]

While Catullus had been seeking an El Dorado in the East, his dear companions, Verannius and Fabullus, had been doing the same in the West. They had vainly tried the province of Spain in the company of Piso,[5] and returned shortly after[6] the arrival of Catullus in Italy, with no better success. This Piso is generally identified with Cn. Calpurnius Piso, who having taken part with Catiline in his first conspiracy, B.C. 66, was hurried off to Spain as Quaestor, with Praetorian authority. This office, we learn from Sallust, (Cat. c. 19,) he did not long hold, having been

[1] xlvi. [2] iv. [3] xxxi.
[4] liii. [5] xxviii. [6] ix., xii., xxviii.

slain while making a progress within his province. Now it is abundantly evident, from the poems cited above, that Verannius and Fabullus were in Spain after the return of Catullus. It is therefore certain that it must have been some other Piso who was praetor in Spain at this time.[1]

After the poet's return from Bithynia he met and deeply loved the beautiful and dissolute Lesbia. A statement of the evidence that has led us to the conclusion that this was the period of his intimacy with that lady may not be inapposite. In the lines addressed to Mamurra's mistress, (xliii.,) written evidently as much for the purpose of ridiculing Mamurra's extravagance as his sweetheart's ugliness, and which one cannot conceive as written prior to Caesar's occupancy of Gaul, (or what is the point in the words "decoctor" and "Provincia"?) she is said to be compared to his matchless Lesbia. But Caesar did not obtain the province of Gaul till B.C. 59, nor set out for it till B.C. 58. The third stanza of Carm. xi. points still more clearly to a period subsequent to 58 as the time of his intimacy with Lesbia.

We are told by Appuleius[2] that her real name was Clodia. From this circumstance most of the editors

---

[1] xlvii. and note thereto.

[2] Appuleius in *Apologia*. Without at all questioning the veracity of Appuleius, it is but fair to state that he lived 200 years after Ca* 'lus.

of Catullus have rushed to the conclusion that she was the sister of the notorious Publius Clodius Pulcher, and wife of Metellus Celer. This supposition, however, cannot consistently be entertained, as we learn from Catullus himself that her husband was living during their intimacy,[1] while we know that Metellus Celer died in B.C. 59, the year before Catullus set out for Bithynia. With many, too, it has been matter of astonishment that Cicero has been so highly eulogised by Catullus,[2] but this need not excite surprise, seeing that the poet's Lesbia could not have been the victim of his merciless attack.

During the next few years Catullus resided occasionally at Verona,[3] Sirmio,[4] and his Tiburtine villa[5]—for in the neighbourhood of Tibur, like Horace, he had a charming little retreat—but principally in Rome.[6] Many of his occasional poems to his friends, the beautiful address to Sirmio, perhaps his celebrated "Hymenaeus" in honour of Junia and Manlius, and his wildly-grand poem of "Atys," were written about this time. With regard to "Atys," it may be vain even to hazard a conjecture—it is so unlike everything else—but surely it is natural to suppose that the charming nuptial song, redolent of flowers and innocence and bliss, was written in the heyday of his own love.

[1] lxxxiii. [2] xlix. [3] xxxv.
[4] xxxi. [5] xliv. [6] lxviii.a 34.

LIFE OF CATULLUS.

Lesbia was now his all-absorbing attraction. He loves her to distraction. He leaves her, vowing that he will never again feel for her the thrill of passion, or the tender emotion of love. But it is only for a little while. Degraded though she be, he cannot leave her. She binds him fast with her silken fetters, and he becomes again her willing slave. Still she cannot be chaste; and, sinking lower and lower, she disappears from our gaze, leaving the poet's heart bursting with sorrow, yet stirred with an unutterable emotion for the once loved object whom many a sad experience has now taught him to loathe.[1]

Soon after an event occurred which cast a gloom over all his after life—the death of a brother in the Troad.[2] Actuated by the holiest feelings of natural piety he made a pilgrimage to Asia Minor to visit his grave, and pay in a foreign land the last sad offices in accordance with the usage of his ancestors. After bidding his silent ashes an eternal farewell he returned once more to Rome,[3] and then retired to Verona,[4] for a time relinquishing even the society of valued friends, and denying himself the solace of the muse.[5] A promise, however, which he had made to his friend Hortalus,[6] to translate for him the "Hair of Berenice" from Callimachus,[7] calls from him an effusion accompanied by the poem in ques-

---

[1] lviii.   [2] ci.   [3] lxviii.ᵃ 34.   [4] lxviii.ᵃ 27.
[5] lxv. and lxviii.   [6] lxv.   [7] lxvi.

tion; but in this, and two subsequent pieces,[1] he strikes the lyre with a tenderer hand and a sadder heart. From the last of these, addressed to Allius, and numbered lxviii.[b] in our translation, we learn that the poet's possessions are still further enlarged, through that friend's liberality, by a gift of land, a house, and "an easier love" than Lesbia, "if not so fair."[2]

Catullus, deeply wounded though he may have been by the faithlessness of his earlier love, has still a heart, if not as passionately fond, far more firmly balanced, and equally alive to the joys of reciprocated affection. He has now, in great measure, thrown jealousy to the winds, a lesson that to a mind like his must have been hard to learn, and in the case of his present mistress he solaces himself in this wise :—

> " And though she may not live for me alone,
>   Few are the falsehoods of my modest maid,
>   Then let me bear them as to me unknown,
>   Nor like a fool her broken faith parade."[3]

About this time would seem to have been written most of his bitter lampoons, evincing deep personal hate as well as utter detestation of the inhuman vices in the individuals whom he branded. Some of these could well have been spared, and the loss of them

[1] lxviii.[a] and lxviii.[b]   [2] lxviii.[b] 27 and 28.
[3] lxviii.[b] 95-97, &c.

would have been great gain to the reputation of Catullus, inasmuch as they have left an indelible stain on the memory of one of the most gifted and guileless of men.

But to this time, too, the brief autumn of an early age, we are assuredly indebted for his grand heroic legend of "Peleus and Thetis."[1] Thoroughly imbued with the spirit of the Grecian mind, and enabled from two voyages across the Ægean to portray with Homeric precision the places and scenes coming within the range of his subject, he was no less admirably qualified, by his own bitter experience, intensity of feeling, and passionate, sensuous nature, to delineate the perfidy of Theseus, the passion of Ariadne, the sweet, heaven-hued bliss of Peleus and Thetis.

In his later years he witnessed the dying struggles of Roman liberty; he saw the most notorious hypocrites and villains exalted to the highest offices of state; he saw Roman honour become a jest, and, as if the fire in the temple of Vesta were extinguished, the virtue of a Roman matron become an empty name.

With his brother's death fresh in his memory, with such a state of society around him, and probably in failing health,[2] we can almost see him penning the ominous lines against Nonius and Vatinius,[3] in which

---

[1] lxiv.   [2] *Vide* Carm. xxxviii.   [3] liii.

he seems longing to kiss the hand that sooner or later must put a period alike to the most poignant of human sorrows and the most rapturous of human joys.

With regard to his personal appearance, we know nothing. With regard to his parents and his earlier years, from his own pen, we know as little. Mythic story has not, as in the case of more fortunate sons of song, portrayed to us "the young Catullus" with bees swarming on his lips or as cherished by doves on the lonely mountain height, but verily the Muses might have bathed his temples with the dews of Helicon, and the laughing Loves rocked him to rest in rosy bowers of bliss.

For he was a joint nursling of Eros and Erato—an amorous as well as an amatory poet. Of no one could it be said with more propriety, that over his heart was outspread "the bloom of young desire and purple light of love." Those wondrous echoes—the poems addressed to Lesbia—that have no parallel in the literature of any language, emphatically stamp him the poet of passion. Yet there is not one offensive expression in their whole composition. We wish that the same could be said of all his productions. Unfortunately this may not be, and though we deplore the turpitude of many of his lines, yea, many in which we cannot claim for him the accorded privilege of the satirist, we are bound to attribute these blemishes in great measure to a too frank and outspoken disposition, and to the gross licence that was allowed alike to plebeian and patrician in his depraved and dissolute age. It cannot, however, be said that these are the offspring of a low and grovelling nature, or that his moral character was worse than that of the greatest men of his own time, or of the period immediately succeeding.

Moreover, the same objections that are raised against him may be urged with equal force against almost every Roman poet. That the freedom of his verses was assailed even in his own day, and by those of perhaps looser morals than himself, is evident from the lines in defence of his amatory poems.[1] The claim which he there makes to purity of life, and which he elsewhere asserts with terrible earnestness,[2] would tend to show that he had not in his life trespassed beyond at least his own ideas of decorum and morality. He admits that his verses are highly spiced in order that they may have a charm for January as well as May,[3] but he indignantly repels the imputation that his life is tainted and impure.

Nor ought we to forget, and this should give some weight to his statement, that in the brightest period of our own poetic literature habitual impurity of expression was as common as in any period of heathen

[1] xvi.   [2] lxxvi.   [3] xvi. 7, 10, 11.

antiquity. The pages of our early dramatists are stained with expressions as objectionable, and the more unpardonable, in that they are the productions of a Christian age. Yet who would think of attaching to Shakspeare's life the impurity of some of his writings?

But by far the strongest argument in favour of Catullus seems to us to lie in his chivalrous, exalted, and high-toned appreciation of the female character. Lesbia is in his eyes the loveliest thing of earth—the glory of a summer sun—till she deservedly incurs his disfavour. Junia, the bride of his friend Manlius, is fair as the myrtle,[1] unrivalled as the hyacinth,[2] tender as the ivy[3] and the vine,[4] and modest as the blushing rose.[5] So, too, is Ariadne.[6] And what a beauty, and depth, and tenderness in his picture of the lovely and hapless Laodamia![7] No poet has paid a higher tribute to virtuous affection, or sung in tenderer tones the joys of wedded love. Nor is there anywhere else to be found a more unsparing denunciation of gross licentiousness and impious criminality. Even the all-dreaded name of the Imperial Dictator cannot shield him from the fury of his fierce and relentless pen.[8] He is as much a foe to autocracy, on the one hand, as he is to democracy on

---

[1] lxi. 21 seqq. [2] lxi. 93. [3] lxi. 34, 35.
[4] lxi. 106 seqq. [5] lxi. 194, 195. [6] lxiv. 86–90.
[7] lxviii. 33 seqq. [8] xxix., liv., lvii.

the other, nor has he more sympathy with Pompey than with Caesar.[1] They are both in his estimation unscrupulous charlatans, bent on the ruin of the Roman name. Though his poems betray almost no political leanings, we easily see that he is at heart a leal old republican. Anything derogatory to Roman liberty or ancient prestige is met with a burst of fierce indignation or bitter scorn. Nor had he one jot more of sympathy with the hordes of vulgar aspirants for poetic honours,—the wretched poetasters of the age:—

"Saecli incommoda, pessimi poetae."[2]

Yet, singularly free from mean jealousy or malevolence, he was ever ready to extend the hand of fellowship, and to award the meed of approbation to his worthy brethren of the lyre.[3] While he was fastidious in literary matters, he was equally so as to the bearing and demeanour of those into whose company he was casually thrown. In short he had a hearty horror of bores of every description.

The pretty, chattering minx of Varus;[4] the urbane, polished, and witty Suffenus,[5] but who, alas! was never so happy as when writing verses and reciting and admiring his wretched drivel;[6] the black-bearded, white-toothed fop Egnatius,[7] with his everlasting grin;

---

[1] xxix. 25.   [2] xiv. 23.   [3] xxxv., l., xcv
[4] x.   [5] xiv. 19 and xxii.   [6] xxii. 16.
[7] xxxvii. 19 and xxxix. *passim.*

the conceited lawyer Sextianus,[1] with his pestilential speech-book; the napkin-filching Murrucinus,[2] and the cockney Arrius,[3] alike come in for a share of his genial indignation.

Catullus seems to have been fond of retirement; and whether sojourning in the city or in one or other òf his country residences, he kept quite aloof from the cares and bustle of public life, finding a purer enjoyment in the society of men of kindred tastes and studies. Of a generous and impulsive nature, sterling honour, an affectionate and confiding disposition, and a keen relish for innocent social enjoyment, he had many friends with whom he lived on terms of the greatest amity.[4] But he was painfully sensitive. The smallest slight; an undue liberty taken with him or his; nay, a single word in disparagement of himself or his friends, wounded him to the soul. And if his loves and friendships were strong and abiding, his hates were equally so. This his invectives against Caesar, Mamurra, Gellius, Vatinius, Vettius, and Cominius amply attest. He

---

[1] xliv. 10 seqq.   [2] xii.   [3] lxxxiv.

[4] Among his especial friends he reckoned Cornelius Nepos, the historian; Licinius Calvus, orator and brother-poet; Caecilius, the author of a poem on Cybele; Caius Helvidius Cinna, the author of "Smyrna," and one of his companions in his Bithynian expedition; the versatile and accomplished genius Asinius Pollio, the poets Cornificius and Hortalus; Cato, the *littérateur;* Alphenus Varus, the lawyer; Manlius Torquatus, Verannius, Fabullus, and others.

would seem never to have forgiven an injury, except the first faithlessness of Lesbia.

The most trivial neglect or apparent forgetfulness of him hurt his feelings, and drew from his bosom bitter sighs of anguish. But in this respect he was equally careful not to wound the feelings of others. Even the temporary interruption of friendly intercourse, and the delay to fulfil a promise, caused by the death of a dearly-loved brother, must be explained to Hortalus, lest he should deem him regardless of his friendship, or careless in the discharge of a sacred duty.[1]

With a detailed notice of his poems we do not mean here to occupy the reader. We would merely indicate the position which we conceive he holds among Roman poets, and the influence which he exercised over his immediate successors.

Catullus was the first Roman *lyric* poet; at least the first who adapted successfully the ancient Greek measures to the Roman lyre. This fact disproves in some measure the unqualified claims of Horace:—

> "Dicar . . . .
> Princeps Æolium carmen ad Italos
> Deduxisse modos."[2]
>   "Parios ego primus iambos
> Ostendi Latio."[3]

---

[1] lxv. [2] Hor. Od. iii. 30. 10-14. [3] Hor. Epist. i. xix. 23, 24.

But perhaps Horace, in the first of these instances, is alluding to the "Alcaic," which he was the first to introduce, and which became in his hands the vehicle for his noblest thoughts. That Catullus enjoyed great popularity in his own day is abundantly evident, both from the many high eulogies passed upon him by writers of antiquity and from the bitter sneer of his lyric rival—

"Simius iste
Nil praeter Calvum et doctus cantare Catullum."[1]

However, that he is entitled to the superlative eulogium of Niebuhr, "that he was the greatest of all the Roman poets, if we except, perhaps, a few of the earlier ones," is a verdict against which many will protest. Horace alone disputes with him the palm of lyric poetry. Without instituting an invidious comparison, we would merely note the chief characteristics of both; and neither, we think, will lose by being placed in juxtaposition.

Catullus had, more than any other Roman poet, passionate intensity of lyrical conception. Horace possessed "fancy, wit, and humour, in matchless combination." There is greater naturalness and more spontaneity in the former; but there is in the latter more graceful expression and far more artistic skill. Catullus seems to have written every line under the

[1] Hor. Sat. I. x. 18, 19.

influence of some uncontrollable impulse; Horace with great diligence and care. The former was content to imitate the Greek model as he found it; the latter careful to give his imitations a distinctive character by confining himself rigidly to severer rules and more in keeping with a severer tongue.

Yet both, though professed imitators of the Greeks, are thoroughly Roman in spirit. They are, however, in the treatment of their subjects, and even in their modes of thought, essentially distinct, and each is unapproachable in his sphere. They are *magis pares quam similes*—the dawn and the sunset—the first and the last of Roman lyric poets.

But it is not on his lyrical effusions alone that the fame of Catullus rests. Indeed his greatest productions are outside the pale of lyric poetry. "Atys" has no rival in any language. The "Peleus and Thetis," again, has passages of far higher epic sublimity than any other Roman poem. Virgil has not attained the grandeur of the "Ariadne," in the famous episode of "Dido," nor the tender pathos of the parting of Ægeus and Theseus in the interview between Æneas and his sire on the downfall of Ilium. The description of the Bacchants[1] in the same poem, which has furnished Rubens with a subject for his great picture, has, perhaps, more life, freshness, and

---

[1] lxiv. 254–264.

originality than any other passage in Roman epic poetry.

Yet, all this notwithstanding, Catullus has not produced an epic. True, he has given evidence of possessing higher epic power than any Roman poet with whom we are acquainted—nothing more. But the world looks to deeds alone; and while we recognise a loftier power in Catullus, we are constrained to accord to Virgil the well-merited praise of being Rome's great epic poet.

The merits of Catullus, therefore, do not rest on his excellence in one species of poetry; he has essayed many, and he is great in them all. Perhaps the highest tribute to his vast and varied abilities is to be found in the fact that none of his successors in the brilliant Augustan period were above imitating his finest passages. While this statement is amply borne out by the references hereafter cited, it is worth mentioning that Ovid, to whom, perhaps more than to any other Roman writer after Catullus, the Muse was prodigal of her gifts, has no less than four times tried his strength on "Ariadne," once, at least, with singular success.[1]

To sum up briefly: Catullus had not the solemn earnestness, the nobleness of purpose, the heroic grandeur of soul that characterised his great contemporary Lucretius; he had not the wit, humour, fancy, and finish of Horace; he had not the labo-

[1] *Vide* Excurs. to Carm., lxiv.

rious perseverance of Virgil; nor was a mercurial nature like his, perhaps, capable of the sustained exertion and toilsome drudgery of a work like the "Æneid;" but he has proved himself as great a master of the grand and stately hexameter, though his frequent spondaic endings may convey an impression of harshness to an ear habituated to the smoother cadence of Virgil. In his elegiac poems he does not uniformly exhibit the terseness and pathetic tenderness of Tibullus, the refined diction and sparkling ingenuity of Propertius, or the deservedly-admired bell-like recurrent chime of Ovid; nor in his epigrams the piquant smartness and chiselled point of Martial, but in the real elements that constitute *the poet* he is without a rival.

It is not the part of talent, however great, to produce an "Atys" or an "Ariadne." It is the high prerogative of genius.

The loss of his writings that have not reached us is, perhaps—we judge from their titles—of little importance;[1] and what he might have done had length

---

[1] It is certain that several of the poems of Catullus have perished. Verses on love charms, (De Incantamentis,) like those of Theocritus and Virgil, are mentioned by Pliny, and Ithyphallic songs, similar to the fragment numbered xviii., by Terentianus Maurus. Nonius, Servius, and others also refer to passages or expressions not found in the extant writings of Catullus. The "Ciris," commonly printed with the works of Virgil, and the lovely poem "De Vere" or "Pervigilium

of days been vouchsafed to him, cannot affect his position now; but what we do possess could ill have been spared from the literature of his country; and the loss of his sprightly little volume (*lepidum novum libellum*)[1] would not only have deprived us of some of the fairest flowers of ancient verse—the *dulces Musarum foetus*[2] which he loved to foster—but would have left us in almost total obscurity regarding one of the few great names that gave a new phase to Roman poetry, and shed a lustre over the decline of the Roman republic.

Veneris," have been claimed for him by some critics. The former of these exhibits a strong resemblance both in expression and style to the "Peleus and Thetis," and is most probably the work of an imitator of Catullus and Lucretius. The "Vigil" bears unmistakable traces of a later hand. The "Phasma," a farce by the mimographer, Q. Lutatius Catullus or Catulus, and the "Laureolus," probably by Laberius or Naevius, have also been erroneously ascribed to him.

[1] i. 1.   [2] lxv. 3.

I.

TO CORNELIUS NEPOS.

To what dear friend, say, shall I dedicate
    My smart new book, just trimm'd with pumice dry?
    To thee, Cornelius—for, in years gone by,
Thou wast accustom'd my light lays to rate
As something more than trifles—ay, and then,
    When thou, the sole Italian, daredst engage
    To paint in three small volumes every age,
With learnèd, Jove! and with laborious pen.
Wherefore accept my tiny leaves, I pray,
    Such as they are,—and, Patron Goddess, give
    This boon : that still perennial they may live
After a century has roll'd away.

II.

TO LESBIA'S SPARROW.

Sparrow! my darling's joy!
With whom she's wont to toy,
With whom some warm breast-nestling-nook to fill;
    And, to frolic combat firing
    Thee her finger-tip desiring,
To provoke the pricking peckings of thy bill.

    What time my beauteous fair,
    My heart's own darling care,
With some endearing sport would please her will,
    As a tiny consolation,
    Doting love's fond recreation,
That her bosom's fretful smartings may be still.

    With thee, like her, to play,
    And drive sad cares away,
Were dear to me, as to the nimble maid,
    Sung in storied legend olden,
    Was the mellow apple golden,
That her long-engirdled bosom disarray'd.

III.

ON THE DEATH OF THE SPARROW.

YE Graces! mourn, oh mourn!
Mourn, Cupids Venus-borh!
And loveliest sons of earth, where'er ye are!
    Dead is now my darling's sparrow—
    Sparrow of my "winsome marrow,"
Than her very eyes, oh! dearer to her far.

    For 'twas a honey'd pet,
    And knew her well as yet
A mother by her daughter e'er was known:
    Never from her bosom stray'd he,
    Hopping hither, thither play'd he,
Ever piped and chirp'd his song to her alone.

    Now to that dreary bourn
    Whence none can e'er return,
Poor little sparrow wings his weary flight;
    Plague on you! ye grimly-low'ring
    Shades of Orcus, still devouring,
All on earth that's fair and beautiful and bright.

    Ye've ravish'd from my sight
    Her sparrow, her delight!
Oh ruthless deed of bale! woe, woe is me!
    Now thy death, poor little sparrow,
    Doth her heart with anguish harrow,
And her swollen eyes are red with tears for thee.

IV.

DEDICATION OF HIS PINNACE.

That pinnace there, my friends, declares she was the
 fleetest vessel
E'er cut the sea, and never fear'd with wind or wave
 to wrestle:
Whate'er the craft — by oar or sail impell'd — she
 could outvie it;
And she avers the shore of threatening Adria can't
 deny it,
Or yet the island Cyclades, or Rhodes renown'd in
 story,
Or rugged Thrace, Propontis, or the Euxine wild and
 hoary,
Where she — a pinnace now — was erst a leafy wood
 canorous,
Whose vocal foliage often breathed sweet murmurings
 o'er Cytorus.

Pontic Amastris! and Cytorus with the boxtree
 green aye!
The pinnace says these things are known, and known
 to you have been aye;
For from her earliest days she stood your lofty brow
 adorning,
First in your waters dipp'd her oars, and ocean's fury
 scorning,

O'er many a wild sea bore her lord, and saw him
    safely harbour'd ;
Whether the wind fill'd fair both sheets, or larboard
    piped, or starboard,
Nor e'er to shore-gods vow'd a vow, if calm or gale
    had caught her,
From farthest ocean till she reach'd this still lake's
    limpid water.

These days are gone ! now quietly stow'd—old age
    her first disaster—
She dedicates herself to you, twin Pollux and twin
    Castor.

V.

TO LESBIA.

THE while we live, to love let's give
    Each hour, my winsome dearie !
Hence, churlish rage of icy age !
    Of love we 'll ne'er grow weary.

Bright Phoebus dies, again to rise ;
    Returns life's brief light never ;
When once 'tis gone, we slumber on
    For ever and for ever

Then, charmer mine, with lip divine !
  Give me a thousand kisses ;
A hundred then, then hundreds ten,
  Then other hundred blisses.

Lip thousands o'er, sip hundreds more
  With panting ardour breathing ;
Fill to the brim love's cup, its rim
  With rosy blossoms wreathing.

We 'll mix them then, lest to our ken
  Should come our store of blisses,
Or envious wight should know, and blight
  So many honey'd kisses.

VI.

TO FLAVIUS.

Flavius ! unless your cherish'd flame
  Were graceless and ungainly,
From me you could not keep her name,
  You 'd wish to tell me plainly ;
Some hackney'd jade, I 'll take my oath upon it,
Has crazed your head, and you're ashamed to own it.

Your bed, ah ! vainly mute ! with flowers
  And Syrian unguents scented ;

Your cushion in the midnight hours,
  All here and there indented;
Its crazy frame—the ambling and the creaking—
Reveal a tale, the truth too plainly speaking.

While these are there, you're mute in vain;
  And why so lean, unless it
Be true you're with such follies ta'en?
  Come—good or bad—confess it.
You and your love—I wish in song to blaze you,
And to the stars in sprightly verse to raise you.

VII.

TO LESBIA.

Love! when we a-kissing go,
  Dost thou ask what sum suffices?
Tell the countless sands that strew
  Warm Cyrene, land of spices,
'Tween Jove's shrine 'mid desert gloom,
And old Battus' hallow'd tomb;

Count night's silent stars that spy
  Stolen joys of maid and lover;
Give me these, and then I'll cry,
  Hold! love's cup is flowing over:
Curious eye a sum so vast
Cannot count, nor ill tongue blast.

VIII.

TO HIMSELF, ON LESBIA'S INCONSTANCY.

WRETCHED CATULLUS! cease to sigh and whine,
And what has perish'd think no longer thine;
Once thou didst summer in a glorious sun!
When thou in raptures of delight didst run
Where'er thy dear, thy peerless charmer roved;
Loved then as girl by thee shall ne'er be loved.
Then many were the gamesome frolics play'd,
Fond was the youth, and not unfond the maid;
Thine was a charmèd life! thy suns how fair!
She flies thee now—thy lot then bravely bear;
Pursue her not; thy misery cease to feel;
And with determined mind thy courage steel.

Maiden, farewell! Catullus feels no more;
Nor will he ask thy love, denied before;
But thou, when ask'd by none, shalt mourn thy fate.
False one! alas! what sorrows thee await?
Who will now fondly by thy side recline?
Or in whose eyes shalt thou in beauty shine?
Who in thy heart will wake love's eager flame?
Of what fond lover shalt thou boast the name?
Whom shall thy kisses fire with bland delight?
Whose lips shalt thou with panting ardour bite?
Care not, Catullus! cease to think—to feel—
Endure with heart hard as the temper'd steel.

IX.

TO VERANNIUS, ON HIS RETURN FROM SPAIN.

Verannius! of my friends before all others
  Though I could count three hundred thousand here,*
Hast thou come home again, thy loving brothers
  And aged mother with thy smile to cheer?

Thou hast. To me most blest of intimations,—
  I'll see thee safe, and hear thee telling o'er
Strange tales of Spanish places, deeds, and nations,
  With all the accustom'd glee thou hadst of yore.

I'll clasp thy neck in tenderest embraces,
  I'll fondly kiss thy pleasant mouth and eyne;
O! all ye happiest of happy faces,
  Where is there joy or happiness like mine?

X.

ON THE MISTRESS OF VARUS.

Friend Varus dragged me off his love to see,
  As I the Forum left quite free from duty;
A girl, as at a glance appear'd to me,
  Devoid of neither sprightliness nor beauty.

---

* Or, if by *millibus trecentis*, 300,000 *sesterces* be meant—
  Verannius! of my friends before all others!
  Millions were nought compared with one so dear!

When we arrived, on various themes we fell,
　Discussed, 'mong others which the occasion offer'd,
Bithynia—how things went there—and, as well,
　What heaps of wealth I there had safely coffer'd.

" Nor I, nor captains, nor their train," I said,
　And spoke the truth, nor ever tried to cheat her,
" Could now display a better scented head,
　Especially with such a knavish praetor

As ours, who prized his cohort not one hair."
　" But surely, sir," thus the sly wanton prated,
" You'd have some slaves to bear your litter there?
　'Tis said the custom there originated."

I to the wench a lucky dog to seem,
　Replied, " Oh, no! my fate was not so bitter,
That, bad although I did the province deem,
　I had not eight straight men to bear my litter."

But neither here nor there, if truth be said,
　Was I of ev'n a single slave the holder,
The broken foot of my old truckle-bed
　To hoist aloft and place upon his shoulder.

Then she, like all her bland seductive train:
　" A little, dear Catullus, let me borrow
Those fellows; I'd so like just to be ta'en
　To great Serapis' temple, say, to-morrow."

"Pardon me, dearest girl; of what I said
 Was mine I'd frankly been to you the donor;
But I was wrong; I fear you've been misled—
 They're Caius Cinna's—madam—he's their owner.

But, whether his or mine, what's that to me?
 I use the fellows just as if I'd bought 'em;
But you will so absurd and plaguy be,
 One cannot tell a fib but you have caught him."

XI.

TO FURIUS AND AURELIUS.

THE FAREWELL MESSAGE TO LESBIA.

O Furius and Aurelius! comrades sweet!
 Who to Ind's farthest shore with me would roam,
Where the far-sounding Orient billows beat
 Their fury into foam;

Or to Hyrcania, balm-breath'd Araby,
 The Sacian's or the quiver'd Parthian's land,
Or where seven-mantled Nile's swoll'n waters dye
 The sea with yellow sand;

Or cross the lofty Alpine fells, to view
 Great Caesar's trophied fields, the Gallic Rhine,
The paint-smear'd Briton race, grim-visaged crew,
 Placed by earth's limit line;

To all prepared with me to brave the way,
    To dare whate'er the eternal gods decree—
These few unwelcome words to her convey
                Who once was all to me.

Still let her revel with her godless train,
    Still clasp her hundred slaves to passion's thrall,
Still truly love not one, but ever drain
                The life-blood of them all.

Nor let her more my once-fond passion heed,
    For by her faithlessness 'tis blighted now,
Like flow'ret on the verge of grassy mead
                Crush'd by the passing plough.

XII.

TO ASINIUS.

ASINIUS! o'er the wine and 'mid the jesting,
    You with your left hand play a shameful part,
Your careless friends of handkerchiefs divesting,
    Think you, poor silly fool! that this is smart?

You do not know how mean 'tis and ungallant!
    Believest not? Ask your brother Pollio, who,
If you'd desist, would gladly give a talent;
    And he's in pleasantries surpass'd by few.

Wherefore expect no end of lashing satire,
   Or now at once my handkerchief resign :
With me the intrinsic value's not the matter,
   But 'tis a *keepsake* from a friend of mine.

Some time ago, Verannius and Fabullus
   Sent me some Saetab handkerchiefs from Spain ;
Their gift it is but right their friend Catullus
   Should prize as dearly as the valued twain.

———◆———

XIII.

TO FABULLUS.

INVITATION TO DINNER.

If the gods will, Fabullus mine,
With me right heartily you'll dine,
Bring but good cheer—that chance is thine
      Some days hereafter ;
Mind a fair girl, too, wit, and wine,
      And merry laughter.

Bring these—you'll feast on kingly fare—
But bring them—for my purse—I swear
The spiders have been weaving there ;
      But thee I'll favour
With a pure love, or, what's more rare,
      More sweet of savour,

An unguent I'll before you lay
The Loves and Graces t' other day
Gave to my girl—smell it—you'll pray
    The gods, Fabullus,
To make you turn all nose straightway.
    Yours aye, Catullus.

XIV.

TO LICINIUS CALVUS.

AT more even than my eyes did I not rate thee,
    Calvus! most pleasant of all friends of mine,
With even Vatinian hatred I would hate thee,
    For that most execrable gift of thine.

What have I done? what word unguarded spoken?
    That thou shouldst plague me with such cursèd trash;
Heaven send that client many an angry token,
    Who sent thee such a store of balderdash!

If, as I'm thinking, your pedantic neighbour
    Sulla sends you this present fresh and choice,
I am not sorry that your valued labour
    Is thus rewarded, nay, I do rejoice.

Great gods! the volume I have now before me
    You've sent your friend—Oh! horrid, cursèd lays!
That all day long the hated sight might bore me
    Upon the Saturnalia, best of days.

No, my fine wag! you'll not get off so easy,
    For with the dawn I'll to the bookstalls hie,
Rifle each nook and shelf—the Aquinii, Caesi,
    Suffenus, all such poison dire I'll buy,

And with these tortures back again I'll pay you.
    Hence, then, vile trash! hence, fare-ye-well the while!
Begone! your cursèd steps retrace, I pray you,
    Scum of the age! bards vilest of the vile!

XV.

TO AURELIUS.

My love I to thy care commend,
    I ask this modest favour;
If e'er thou hadst a darling friend,
    And yearn'dst from shame to save her,

O! tend this girl with tenderest care,
    I'm easy altogether
'Bout those who throng the thoroughfare
    And hurry hither, thither;

But 'tis thyself—thy wiles I fear,
   Each maiden's fame destroying;
So, to some other market steer,
   If needs thou must be toying;

For, if I find thy lustful heart
   Has led thee to misuse her,
I swear thou'lt from the torments smart
   Reserved for the seducer.

XVI.

TO AURELIUS AND FURIUS.

Base Furius and Aurelius! hence, away!
   Who think that I'm unchaste because my verses
Breathe tales of tender love and harmless play;
Chaste should the modest bard himself be aye,
   Not so the amorous themes his muse rehearses.

'Tis when his lines with tender fervour flow,
   And thrill the soul like an inspiring potion,
That they possess the genuine spice and glow,
Firing not youth alone, but age, whose slow
   And frozen limbs are well-nigh reft of motion.

Because ye've read some lay of mine of late,
   Wherein I sang of many thousand kisses,

Ye think me wanton and effeminate.
Avaunt! or yours will be a dreadful fate,
  The poet's lash is one that seldom misses.

XVII.

TO A CERTAIN TOWN.

(Rendered into English after the original verse.)

Town! O Town, that desirest on thy long bridge to exhibit
Sports, and yearnest to trip in the dance, but fear'st the weak timber
Props of thy little rickety bridge, lest, falling supinely
Past remead, it should lie overwhelm'd in quagmire abysmal,
So to thee be a capital bridge—the dream of thy fancy—
One on which may be ventured the rites of Salian dancers.
Then, O Town! to me grant this rare boon of merriest laughter:
List, a townsman of mine, I wish from thy bridge I could headlong
Hurl, and duck in the marsh below, heels o'er head in its waters,
Ay! and there, where, of all the abyss and dark slimy cesspool,

Yawns the sink of corruption by far the blackest and deepest.
Oh! but he is an ass, nor as wise as two-year-old infant,
Hush'd and rock'd to repose on the trembling arm of his father,
Mated, too, with a beauteous girl—sweet flower in her springtide,
Tenderer far than the tenderest youngling kid of the meadows,
Needing warier 'tendance than lush-black grapes on the vine-branch :
Yet he leaves her to romp as she will, not one straw he careth,
Ne'er bestirs he himself in the least, but lies like an alder,
Fell'd by tree-lopper's axe in a ditch of woody Liguria,
Wholly blind and obtuse as if she were nothing or nowhere.
Such a dolt is this townsman of mine, he sees not, he hears not.
Sooth! he knoweth not whether he is or really is not.
Now I wish from the top of thy bridge to pitch him head-foremost,
Just to find out if suddenly one might rouse the dull numscull,
And leave fast in the glutinous mire his spirit insensate,
Even as leaveth the hinny its iron shoe in the gutter.

XVIII.

TO THE GARDEN GOD.

To thee this grove I dedicate and consecrate, Priapus,
Who hast thy shrine and shady wood at Lampsacus, Priapus,
For chiefly in its towns the Hellespont thy glory soundeth,
Than which no other shelly shore in oysters more aboundeth.

XIX.

THE GARDEN GOD.

My lads! this farm, this cottage by the mead,
Thatched with the willow-wand and rushy reed,
I, a dry oak, by rude axe shapen, cheer
With blessings richer each returning year.
The poor cot's owner and his little boy
Revere and hail me as their god with joy,
The sire with constant diligence proceeds
To clear my fane of rough and prickly weeds,
The son with anxious care large gifts bestows—
From his small hand the offering ever flows.
Spring's firstlings on my fane are duly laid,
The flower-streak'd wreath, soft ear, and tender blade;
Posies of yellow violets are mine;

The saffron poppy decorates my shrine;
The fragrant apple and the pale-green gourd;
And lush-red grapes 'neath shady leaves matured.
Oft—breathe it not—upon my fane has bled
The bearded goat, or horn-hoof'd spouse instead;
For all these gifts is not Priapus bound
To watch his master's vines and garden ground?
Then hence, my lads! keep off your thievish hands,
Our nearest neighbour there is rich in lands;
And his Priapus has a careless air,
Go, take from him. This path will lead you there.

XX.

THE GARDEN GOD.

I, TRAVELLER, a dry poplar rudely wrought,
    Guard on the left this little plot of land,
Its humble owner's garden and his cot,
    And keep away the thief's rapacious hand.

Spring round my brow a flowery garland twines;
    Summer the ear embrown'd by Phoebus' power;
Autumn the verdant lush-grape-cluster'd vine;
    The olive pale is icy winter's dower.

The tender goat within my pastures fed,
    Her well-fill'd udder bears to yonder town;
The fatted lambkin from my sheepfolds led,
    With heavy gold the cotter's care doth crown.

The gentle calf, while lows its mother here,
   Stains with its blood the fane of deity :
Then, traveller, this god thou shalt revere,
   And keep thy hands <u>aloof</u>; 'twere well for thee ;

For I've a weapon here might do thee harm.
   Come on, you say, I'd like to see you try;
Lo ! here the cotter comes, whose sturdy arm
   Can wield the club I'll readily supply.

XXI.

TO AURELIUS.

AURELIUS ! bleak starvation's sire,
   In present, past, or future day,
And thou, inflamed by foul desire,
     Wouldst wean my love away !

Nor secretly : for soon as e'er
   Thou 'rt with her, thou beginn'st to smile,
To jest, caress her, and ensnare
     Her heart with every wile.

In vain : I'll to the world proclaim
   Thy faithless and insidious ways,
If thou shouldst dare her spotless fame
     To sully and debase.

If thou in pamper'd ease and state
  Didst this, I then might silent be;
But, oh! I mourn my darling's fate,
  To starve and thirst with thee.

Then cease, whilst still thou canst command
  A modest and unsullied name,
Or thou shalt wear the ignoble brand
  Of perfidy and shame.

XXII.

TO VARUS.

Varus! that youth Suffenus whom you know
Is quite a clever and accomplish'd beau—
Can pleasantly on any theme converse,
Is witty, too, and writes no end of verse.
I verily believe he's written o'er
A round ten thousand lines perhaps, or more;
Not done, as usual, on palimpsest,
No, but on royal paper, and the best,
New boards, new bosses, bands of richest red,
The sheets with pumice smooth'd and ruled with lead.
When these you read, the beau, the wit is dead;
A goatherd or a ditcher's left instead;
Such is the difference—so vast the change!
How then explain a thing so very strange?
The man whom now the prince of wits we see,
Or glibber still, if aught more glib there be,

Becomes more boorish than a boorish clown
Whene'er to poesy he settles down;
What's more, he never half so happy seems
As when he's writing his poetic themes;
His joy unbounded tongue could ne'er express,
He so admires his wondrous cleverness.
Doubtless we're all mistaken so—'tis true,
Each is in something a Suffenus too:
Our neighbour's failing on his back is shown,
But we don't see the wallet on our own.

XXIII.

TO FURIUS.

Furius! of neither slave nor chest,
Nor spider, bug, or fire possest,
A sire and step-dame thine alone,
Whose teeth can masticate the stone.
Fair is thy lot in such a house,
With him and with his wooden spouse!
No wonder: health your days doth cheer,
Ye've good digestion, nought to fear,
No fire, nor baleful ruins there,
No impious deeds, nor poison's snare,
Mishaps and dangers both ye scorn,
Ye've bodies drier far than horn,
Or aught, if aught more dry there be,
From heat, or cold, or poverty,
Why not live well and happily?

From thee no sweat or spittle flows,
Mucus or moisture from your nose;
In fine, a match for thee, I ween,
In cleanliness was never seen.
A life with boons so precious fraught,
Oh! ne'er despise nor rate at naught;
For money never breathe a prayer,
For you of blessings have your share.

XXIV.

TO A BEAUTY.

O LOVELIEST flow'ret! Beauty's peerless queen
In this our age, or that the past hath seen,
Or that shall blossom in an after day!
I'd rather thou hadst thrown my all away
On that low wretch, who has nor slave nor chest,
Than let thyself be thus by him caress'd.
" How? is he not a beau?" you'll say.—He's so;
But neither slave nor purse has this fine beau.
My counsel, if you will, reject, disdain :
He has nor slave nor chest I still maintain.

XXV.

TO THALLUS.

BASE THALLUS! softer far than rabbit's hair,
Than goose's marrow, or than tip of ear,
Than flabby feeble age, or spider's airy snare.

Yet thou, the self-same Thallus, art even more
Rapacious than the driving storm, whose roar
Scares wild on fluttering wing the gape-mouth'd birds
    ashore.

Send back my cloak and Saetab kerchief, pray,
And Thynian tablets thou hast filch'd away,
Which thou, like heirlooms, fool! dost openly display.

Unglue them from thy nails and give them back,
Lest the dread lash should scar with smarting crack
Thy back and tender flanks with many an ugly track,

And thou shouldst toss and boil excessively,
Like tiny craft caught in the mighty sea
When round the wild winds rave with mad tempes-
    tuous glee.

XXVI.

TO FURIUS.

FURIUS! my villa is not *set*, I find,
Against the north, south, west, or eastern wind;
But O! a wind more dread, more baleful still,
A fifteen thousand, ten score sesterce bill!

XXVII.

TO HIS CUPBEARER.

YOUNG server of the old Falernian wine!
Pour drier liquor in this cup of mine;
Postumia rules our festive board to-night—
'Tis her command—be it observed aright;
And, sooth, she likes the purple juice more strong
Than ever drunken grape-seed lay among.
Then, cooling waters! hence where'er ye please,
Hence! bane of wine, to spoil my beaker cease,
Go, seek a while the sober and severe :
The pure Thyonian only sparkles here.

XXVII.

TO HIS CUPBEARER.

(ANOTHER VERSION.)

YOUNG server of old Falern! ho!
   Pour drier cups for me,
Our queen Postumia wills it so,
   Be sacred her decree.

For as the tipsy grape-stone sips
   The juice that round it rolls,
So revel gay Postumia's lips
   In nectar-brimming bowls.

Then, water, hence where'er ye will,
    Thou bane of rosy wine!
Go, seek the sober: here we swill
    Thyonian juice divine.

XXVIII.

TO VERANNIUS AND FABULLUS.

Piso's suite! come, tell Catullus,
    You with knapsacks neat and light,
Dear Verannius and Fabullus,
    Has your business gone all right?
Have you with that famine-monger
Borne enough of cold and hunger?

What in shape of gains expended
    Show your ledgers in the gross?
While my praetor I attended,
    I—I tell you—gain'd a loss.
Memmius! ah! you rogued me finely,
Screwed me—held me down supinely.

But, as far as I can judge on
    This point, you were much the same;
No whit better your curmudgeon;
    Cringe to friends of noble name!
Heaven send ills without cessation
On such miscreants of the nation!

XXIX.

ON MAMURRA, ADDRESSED TO CAESAR.

Who can see it? who can bear it?
    But a rake and gamester vile,
That Mamurra should inherit
    Gaul and distant Britain's isle?
Wilt thou see and bear the while?
Caesar! rake! leech! gamester vile!

Shall that proud and pamper'd minion
    To the beds of all repair,
Like the dove of snowy pinion,
    Or Adonis young and fair?
Wilt thou see and bear the while?
Caesar! rake! leech! gamester vile!

Didst thou seek, unique commander!
    That far island of the west,
But to glut that batter'd pander?
    "What is all he spends at best?"
Cries your ill-placed bounty, "Hey!
'Tis a trifle"—is't then, pray?

First his father's hoards devouring,
    Then the plunder Pontus gave,
Then the wealth that Spain sent showering
    From the Tagus' golden wave.
Now his dreaded name appals
Both the Britons and the Gauls.

Why then nurse this odious creature?
    What to you can he avail
  But to sponge you and to eat your
    Fat possessions tooth and nail?
  Drain'd ye all to glut his maw,
  Sire-in-law and son-in-law!

XXX.

TO ALPHENUS.

ALPHENUS! faithless to thy trust! false to thy comrades leal!
Dost thou for thy fond friend, hard-hearted one! no sorrow feel?
To wrong and to betray me, wretch! each chance thou 'rt quick to seize,
Yet false men's impious deeds will ne'er the blest immortals please.

But this thou sett'st at nought and leav'st me wretched, whelm'd in woes;
Alas! what now can mortals do? in what man faith repose?
Surely thou badest me yield my soul, perfidious one! to thee,
Leading me into love, as if all things were safe to me;

Now thou forsak'st me, and thy words and actions all
    are given
An empty offering to the winds and airy blasts of
    heaven;
If thou forgett'st, not so the gods,—yea, Faith remem-
    bers too,
Who'll make thee in an after day thy shameful con-
    duct rue.

XXXI.

TO THE PENINSULA OF SIRMIO, ON HIS RETURN TO HIS VILLA THERE.

Of all peninsulas and isles,
    Set in clear lake or sea,
By twin-realm'd Neptune girt with smiles,
    The eye must Sirmio be!

As, joyful, on thy shore I stand,
    I scarce can think I'm free
From Thynia and Bithynia's land,
    And gazing safe on thee.

Oh! what more blessèd than to find
    Release from all our cares!
When layeth down the weary mind
    The burden that it bears:

When, all our toil of travel o'er,
   Our hearth again we tread,
And lay us down in peace once more
   On the long-wish'd-for bed.

Prize for a world of labours meet,
   Worth all the weary while!
Be glad, sweet Sirmiö! and greet
   Thy master with a smile.

Laugh, all ye Lydian waves, I come!
   Your joy my herald be!
And send the rippling welcome home,
   That all may laugh with me.

XXXII.

TO IPSITHILLA.

My heart's delight, my darling sprite,
   Sweet Ipsithilla! prithee,
Command that I to thee may hie,
   To pass the noontide with thee.

And if by thee I'm bid, then see
   Thy door unbarrèd be, love!
Nor wish to roam away from home,
   But stay and gladden me, love!

Caresses rare for me prepare,
   Be three times three the number;
For here alone, I yearn, mine own,
   To clasp thee ere I slumber.

Now luncheon's o'er, delay no more,
   Say come, and I shall fill a
Deep goblet rare to thee, my fair,
   My charming Ipsithilla.

XXXIII.

ON THE VIBENNII.

OF all the smart thieves at the baths, there's not one,
Vibennius, like thee—none so base as thy son!
The father far-famed for his thievish right hand!
The son the most infamous scamp in the land!
Then why not at once to the mischief be gone?
Your thefts to the people are very well known;
And your son is so thoroughly steep'd in disgrace,
No man will employ him who looks at his face.

XXXIV.

HYMN TO DIANA.

We share Diana's guardian care.
   Maidens and youths, a spotless throng !
We, spotless youths and maidens fair,
         Her praises raise in song.

O mighty child of mightiest Jove !
   Thee, great Diana ! we adore,
Whom, near the Delian olive-grove,
         The fair Latona bore,

That thou shouldst be the Virgin Queen
   Of mountain and of verdant wood,
Of the sequester'd valley green,
         And river's roaring flood.

In woman's hour of travail, thou
   Art hail'd Lucina in her prayers ;
Trivia ; and Luna when thy brow
         A borrow'd splendour wears.

In monthly periods, Goddess ! still
   The rolling year thou dost allot,
And with a bounteous hand dost fill
         The peasant's humble cot.

Whatever name by thee is held
　　Most sacred, be it ever thine!
And guard, as in the years of eld,
　　　　Rome and her ancient line.

XXXV.

TO CAECILIUS.

PAPER! to my friend Caecilius,
　　Tender bard, this message take,
Bid him for a while New Como
　　And the Larian shore forsake.
Bid him hasten to Verona,
　　Say I've something in his line,
That he'll hear some cogitations
　　Of a friend of his and mine.

Wherefore, if he's wise, he'll hurry
　　Over hill and thorough glen,
Though his charmer fair a thousand
　　Times should call him back again,
And, around his neck entwining
　　Both her arms, implore delay,
For 'tis said she for him yearneth
　　With a desperate love alway.

Since he read to her his legend
　　Of the Dindymenian dame,

Through the poor child's inmost marrow
  Burneth love's consuming flame.
I forgive thee, maid more learnèd
  Than the Sapphic muse of old,
For in lovely strains Caecilius
  Hath the mighty Dame extolled.

―――◆―――

XXXVI.

ON THE ANNALS OF VOLUSIUS.

LAYS Volusian! lays most stupid!
  For my charmer pay a vow—
For to Venus blest and Cupid
  She has vow'd if I should now
Just—renewing love's fond plightings—
  Cease my harsh iambic line,
She'd the vilest bard's choice writings
  To the limping god consign,
To be burnt with logs unlucky;
  And my pretty charmer sees
That her vow, so smart and plucky,
  Can be paid with none but these.

Sea-sprung Queen who oft hast eyed us,
  Haunting blest Idalia's grounds,
Syria's plains, Ancona, Cnidus,
  Where the waving reed abounds,

Amathus and Golgos ;—Lady
  Of Dyrrachium, Adria's mart!
Oh, accept the vow she's made ye,
  If it's pretty, if it's smart.
Hence among the embers! shrivel,
  Smoke and smoulder there the while,
Heap of boorishness and drivel,
  Lays Volusian !' paper vile !

XXXVII.

TO THE FREQUENTERS OF A CERTAIN TAVERN.

Ye loose frequenters of that drinking den,
Ninth sign-post from the egg-capp'd brothers' shrine,
And do ye think that ye alone are men,
And have, to kiss the girls, a right divine ?
Or think ye, fools, because ye loiter there,
A hundred, or belike two hundred strong,
That I, though single-handed, will not dare
To thrash the whole two hundred ? then ye're wrong;
Think well on't; for each sot to shame I'll damn
Upon the sign-board in an epigram.
For my own darling who my bosom fled—
Loved as no girl shall e'er be loved by me,
For whom in many a battle fierce I've bled—
Is housed in that low den of infamy.

Ye all caress her, happy souls and blest!
Oh! 'tis too bad—sneaks, scoundrels every one;—
And thou the chief, Egnatius, flowing-tress'd,
The rabbit-warren'd Celtiberia's son,
Whose only merit's that dark beard of thine,
And teeth well-scrubbed with filthy Spanish brine.

XXXVIII.

TO CORNIFICIUS.

O Cornificius! ills and woes
    Upon thy friend Catullus press;
And daily, hourly, deeper grows
        The gloom of his distress.

What word of comfort hast thou brought?—
    A task how easy and how light!—
I feel indignant at the thought
        That thou thy friend wouldst slight.

Oh! dost thou thus my love repay?
    One strain my aching heart might ease,
Though sadder than the tearful lay
        Of sad Simonides.

XXXIX.

ON EGNATIUS.

BECAUSE Egnatius' teeth are white and clear,
He grins always: if pleader draw the tear
When at the bar a criminal's arraign'd,
He grins: if at the pile, with grief unfeign'd,
Reft mother wails her darling only son,
He grins: whate'er the time or place, all one,
He grins: 'tis a disease with him I feel,
Inelegant, I think, and ungenteel.
Then I must warn thee, good Egnatius mine,
Wert thou a Roman, Sabine, Tiburtine,
A frugal Umbrian, fat Etrurian,
Swart, huge-tooth'd Lanuvine, or Transpadan—
Like me—or from a land where people dwell
Who wash their teeth with water from the well,
I'd say renounce thy ceaseless idiot grin,
A silly laugh is folly, if not sin.
Thou'rt Celtiberian: in thy land they say
Each one with a queer lotion, every day,
As regularly as the morning comes,
Is wont to scrub his teeth and russet gums;
Therefore, the more your teeth like ivory shine,
The clearer 'tis you've swill'd the odious brine.

XL.

TO RAVIDUS.

RAVIDUS! wretch! what dark infatuation
  Makes thee fall foul of my iambic lay?
What god at thy unholy invocation
  Prepares to kindle up the frantic fray?
Wouldst be a theme of gossip for the rabble?
  Wouldst thou be famed on any terms? Thou'lt be:
Since with my love of love thou'st dared to gabble,
  Even at the risk of lasting infamy.

———◆———

XLI.

ON THE MISTRESS OF FORMIANUS.

AH me! and did I hear aright?
  Whole sixty pounds did she propose?
  That damsel with the hideous nose,
Spendthrift Mamurra's heart's delight.

Neighbours who for her welfare care
  Her friends and doctors hither call;
  The wench is mad, nor thinks at all,
Or thinks her brazen face is fair.*

* Or, according to the text of *Schwabe*—
    The wench is mad: don't ask at all
    What like she is: she's mad, I'll swear.

XLII.

ON A CERTAIN FEMALE.

Hendecasyllabics! haste
   Hither all; an ugly hack
Thinks to make of me a jest—
   Will not give your tablets back;
If ye can, wield satire's blade,
Come! pursue and dun the jade.

Ask ye who she is? 'tis she
   Strutting there with sluttish jog,
Sillily, disgustingly,
   Grinning like a Gallic dog.
Fence her round, wield satire's blade:
"Give them back, you ugly jade."

Car'st thou nought, O dirt! O slough!
   Baser if aught baser be,
This ye must not think enough:
   If ye've nothing more—let's see—
Surely we a blush can raise
On the gipsy's brazen face.

Shout with louder voice again,
"Give them back, most vile of queans."
Nought she's moved—'tis all in vain:
   You must change the mode and means;
Try, if more can yet be said,
"Give them back, chaste, modest maid."

XLIII.

ON THE MISTRESS OF FORMIANUS.

Hail, maiden! with nor little nose,
  Nor pretty foot, nor jet-black eye,
  Nor fingers long, nor mouth e'er dry,
Nor tongue whence pleasing prattle flows.

You spendthrift Formian's heart engage;
  And doth the province call you fair,
  And Lesbia's charms with yours compare?
O witless and O boorish age!

XLIV.

TO HIS FARM.

My villa! whether call'd by Sabine or Tiburtine name,
For those who hold Catullus dear right sturdily declaim
That thou art on Tiburtine ground, but those who'd wound his heart
Contend, on any terms, that thou a Sabine villa art;
But really whether Tiburtine or Sabine, matters not,
Right gladly did I find myself in thy suburban cot,
And from my chest spat out a grievous cough—not undeserved—
My stomach gave me waiting for a sumptuous dinner served.

For while I was at Sestius' house, at dinner by desire,
He read me an oration full of plague and poison dire,
That he had made against some claimant—Antius was his name—
Then a cold fit and frequent cough shook all my shivering frame,
Until I to thy bosom fled immediate, nothing loth,
And wholly cured myself again with rest and nettle-broth.
Wherefore, to health restored, I give sincerest thanks to thee,
Because in mercy thou hast not avenged my sins on me;
Nor would I greatly grieve, if I should hear his trash again,
To see him in a shivering fit, and coughing might and main.
But not on me—on Sestius let them fall for his misdeed,
Who ne'er invites me but when he has some vile trash to read.

XLV.

ON ACME AND SEPTIMIUS.

Septimius clasp'd unto his breast
   His Acme—his delight—
"My Acme," he the maid address'd,
   And thus his faith did plight:

ON ACME AND SEPTIMIUS.

"If mine be not a desperate love,
That through all after years will prove
Unchanged, unchill'd while life remains,
May I alone on Lybia's plains,
Or scorching India's arid land,
Before the green-eyed lion stand."
 To hear him, Love, as ever, pleased,
 From left to right approval sneezed.

His Acme then, in loving guise,
 Back gently bent her head,
Kiss'd her sweet boy's love-drunken eyes
 With rosy lip, and said:
"So, Septimillus! life! mine own!
Be ever thou my lord alone,
And mine the more, as still more dire
In my soft marrow burns love's fire."
 To hear her, Love, as ever, pleased,
 From left to right approval sneezed.

With mutual love beloved, the pair
Start on life's path with omens fair,
The love-sick youth prefers her smile
To Syria's realms and Britain's isle;
In him alone his Acme true
Finds joys and pleasures ever new.
Who e'er hath seen, the world around,
A love with happier auspice crown'd?

XLVI.

TO HIMSELF, ON THE RETURN OF SPRING.

Now Spring, returning, comes with genial gales,
    The equinoctial fury of the sky
Before the balmy breath of zephyr quails.
    Catullus! bid the Phrygian fields good-bye,
And, leaving warm Nicaea's fertile land,
Speed to where Asia's famous cities stand.

Even now my fluttering heart begins to feel
    Fond fancy's soft anticipating swell;
My joyful feet are quick with new-born zeal;
    Ye sweet companions of my youth, farewell!
We, who together left our distant home,
Homeward by various ways diversely roam.

XLVII.

TO PORCIUS AND SOCRATION.

O Porcius and Socration! each the minion
    Of Piso—scum and starvelings of the land!
Do ye in that low profligate's opinion
    Before Verannius and Fabullus stand?
Do ye feast daily upon dainty meats,
While they must hunt for biddings in the streets?

XLVIII.

ON A BEAUTY.

The honey'd eyes of one so fair
  Could I but press for ever,
Three hundred thousand kisses there
  I'd print, and tire, oh! never,
Though more than autumn's dry ears were
  The kisses I should give her.

XLIX.

TO CICERO.

Tully, most eloquent of all the line
Of Romulus, past, present, or to be,
Catullus sends sincerest thanks to thee,
Poorest of bards—as far the poorest he
As thou art first in eloquence divine.

L.

TO LICINIUS.

Dear Licinius, at our leisure
    Much we sported yesterday;
Wrote, as suited men of pleasure,
    On my tablets many a lay.
Each, o'er every measure ranging,
    Penn'd in play the polish'd line,
Mutual sallies interchanging,
    'Mid the joke and o'er the wine.

And I left you so excited
    With your wit and jollity,
I no more in food delighted,
    Nor in sleep could close an eye;
Wayward frenzy kept me waking,
    In my bed I tumbled o'er,
Yearning for the day-dawn breaking,
    To be with my friend once more.

But, when lay my limbs toil-weary,
    In a half-lethargic state,
I this ditty spun, my cheery
    Friend, to tell you of my fate;
Be not proud, nor spurn, I pray you,
    Apple of mine eye! my prayer,
Lest stern Nemesis repay you.
    She is fierce: beware! beware!

LI.[a]

TO LESBIA.

GODLIKE to me that youth appears,
   Yea, more than god, if more may be,
   Who, seated face to face with thee,
Thy dulcet laughter sees and hears;

Ah, wretched me! of sense bereft,
   For, when I cast on thee a glance,
   To me the power of utterance,
O Lesbia, is no longer left.

Freezes my tongue; through nerve and limb.
   The subtle flame electric veers;
   Unbidden tingle both mine ears;
Mine eyes in seas of darkness swim;

[Soul-chilling sweats adown me pour;
   Cold shiverings through my vitals pass;
   And I am greener than the grass,
And breathless seem to live no more.]

LI.ᵇ

Ease, O Catullus, ruin brings,
  Ease is thy joy and chief delight,
  Ease hath erewhile in rayless night
Entomb'd proud states and mighty kings.

LII.

TO HIMSELF, ON STRUMA AND VATINIUS.

Catullus, why life's burden longer bear?
Now Struma Nonius fills the curule chair,
And, by the consulship, the blackest lie
Vatinius swears: why live, Catullus, why?

LIII.

ON SOMEBODY AND CALVUS.

I laugh'd at a man in the crowd t' other day,
  Who, as Calvus was lustily trouncing
Vatinius, and wondrously well, sooth to say,
  Was the crimes of the scoundrel denouncing;
Cried, uplifting his hands, and with wonder nigh dumb:
" Mighty gods! what an eloquent hop-o'-my-thumb."

LIV.

TO CAESAR.

COARSE CAESAR! would that Otho's puny pate,
And half-wash'd Vettius, and lewd Libo's prate,
If nothing else, might thy displeasure gain,
And that of old Fuffetius, young again:
Once more from my iambics thou shalt wince;
They 're honest, ne'ertheless, most noble prince.

LV.

TO CAMERIUS.

(FROM THE TEXT OF DOERING.)

IF I should not be irksome thought,
    Pray tell me where you hide?
The Campus, Circus I have sought,
    And every bookstall tried,
Traversed immortal Jove's right sacred fane,
And Pompey's portico, but all in vain.

My friend, I every girl address'd
    Who wore a smile serene,
"Where is Camerius?"—hard I press'd—
    "Come, tell, you wicked quean;"
And one her bosom all unveiling said:
"He lurks between these nipples rosy-red."

'Twere toil Herculean thee to tear
   From such a favour'd seat,
No wonder you're from home you swear,
   Come tell me your retreat;
Out with it boldly in the face of day,
Or do the milk-white maidens hold you, pray?

If in close mouth you keep your tongue,
   You spoil love's every fruit,
For Venus joys to dwell among
   Love-tattle, then, why mute?
Still, if you will, be silent evermore,
But let me share your friendship as before.

Were I the guardian lord of Crete,
   If Pegasus me bore,
If Ladus I, or Perseus fleet,
   Who wingèd sandals wore,
Did I the white swift team of Rhesus rein,
Or match the feather-footed flying twain,

Or were the rapid fury mine
   Of winds that scour the air;—
In seeking for that haunt of thine
   My marrow I'd outwear;—
Devour'd by many languors I would be,
Friend of my heart! in searching after thee.

LVI.

TO CATO.

Here's a joke well worth hearing, my Cato,
   A thing full of humour and fun,
If you love me I pray you give way to
   A good hearty laugh when I've done.

I've just caught a young rascal decoying
   My sweetheart with speeches so fine,
While she sat beside him enjoying
   His glances as if they'd been mine.

Venus! goddess to lovers still dearest,
   My passion I could not contain,
So I just took the weapon was nearest,
   And pommell'd him well with my cane.

LVII.

TO MAMURRA AND CAESAR.

Disgraceful Mamurra and Caesar! bright stars!
   In vice ye are charmingly suited,
No wonder: ye both on your face wear the scars,
One of Roman and t'other of Formian wars,
   Indelibly stamp'd and deep-rooted.

Diseased both alike, alike twin-brothers rare,
  Bedfellows, both learnèd reputed,
Alike ye shine forth an adulterous pair,
Twin rivals alike for the smiles of the fair,
  In vice, oh, how charmingly suited!

———◆———

LVIII.

TO COELIUS, CONCERNING LESBIA.

COELIUS, my Lesbia, Lesbia who of yore
  Shone first in every charm and winning grace,
She whom alone Catullus prized before
  His very self, yea, even all his race,
Now in the open street and narrow lane
Barters with Rome's proud sons her charms for gain.

———◆———

LIX.

ON RUFA AND RUFULUS.

DOES Rufulus, then, the prim coxcomb, carouse
With Bononian Rufa, Menenius' spouse?
That wretch you've oft seen in the graveyards erewhile
A-stealing a meal from the funeral pile,

And who, filching the bread that roll'd down from
    the flame,
Was beat by the half-shaved corse-burner? The
    same.

LX.

FRAGMENT.

OF lioness on Lybia's mountains roaming,
Or barking Scylla with mad fury foaming,
    Art thou the dark-soul'd son?
That thou couldst hear a suppliant's voice, despising
His cries for help and shrieks heart-agonising,
    Too cruel-hearted one!

LXI.

NUPTIAL SONG IN HONOUR OF JUNIA AND MANLIUS.

HABITANT of Helicon!
    Offspring of Urania fair!
Thou who bear'st the tender bride
To the loving bridegroom's side,
    O Hymen! hear our prayer!

With sweet-odour'd marjoram flowers
    Wreathe thy beauty-radiant brow;
Seize the veil of flame-bright hue;
Joyous come with saffron shoe
    Upon thy foot of snow.

Rouse thee on the gladsome day!
    Chanting nuptial strains divine,
Let thy silvery voice resound;
Foot it nimbly: brandish round
    The torch of blazing pine.

Junia comes to Manlius,
    As Idalian Venus came
To the judge on Ida's height—
Comes, a maid with auspice bright,
    And pure unsullied name,

Like an Asian myrtle fair—
    All its branchlets gemm'd with flowers!
Which the Hamadryad girls
Nurse with morning's dewy pearls—
    A plaything in their bowers.

Come, then! here thy footsteps bear,
    Haste to leave the Aonian caves
Of the rocky Thespian hill,
Which cool Aganippe's rill
    With crystal waters laves.

Summon home the happy bride,
   Yearning with her lord to be,
Bind her soul with love's strong strings,
As the clasping ivy clings,
   Here, there, all round the tree.

Spotless maidens! swell the train:
   Equal bliss ye soon shall know,
On a like auspicious day:
Carol loud the measured lay,
   O Hymen! Hymen, O!

That, when hearing he is call'd
   To his office, he may prove
Favouring, nor turn aside,
Leading here a virtuous bride,
   And blending hearts in love.

Whom should lovers more invoke—
   More invoke in weal or woe?
Whom in heaven shall men with more
Heartfelt reverence adore?
   O Hymen! Hymen, O!

For his daughters oft the sire
   Calls on thee with loving fear:
Maidens loose for thee the zone:
And the bridegroom hears alone
   Thy name with eager ear.

On the passion-burning youth,
   Blooming girl thou dost bestow,
From the doting mother's breast,
Hymenaeus! god thrice blest!
   O Hymen! Hymen, O!

Venus but for thee achieves
   Nought deserving honour fair:
Lend but thou a willing ear,
She with every gift can cheer:
   Who dares with thee compare?

Homes are childless but for thee;
   For the father smiles no son
Who with heirs his line may swell:
Will it thou, and all is well:
   O Hymen, peerless one!

Where thy rites are unobserved,
   Never guardian souls are given
O'er the godless land to dwell:
Will it thou, and all is well:
   Thou peerless child of heaven!

Hark! the virgin comes along,
   Throw the barr'd gates open wide:
See the flambeaux' lustrous trains!
But thou tarriest; daylight wanes:
   Come forth! come forth, young bride!

Maiden shame her step retards,
    Though she's eager, flows the tide
Of tears, that she must go away;
But thou tarriest; pales the day:
    Come forth! come forth, young bride !

O Aurunculeïa,
    Weep not: there's no fear for thee,
That a fairer maiden may
View the glorious orb of day
    Uprising from the sea.

So, in rich lord's garden ground,
    Deck'd with flowers on every side,
The hyacinth unrivall'd reigns;
But thou tarriest; daylight wanes:
    Come forth! come forth, young bride !

If it seemeth fit to thee,
    Youthful bride! no longer bide;
Come and hear our nuptial strains:
See the flambeaux' golden manes!
    Come forth! come forth, young bride !

Never, faithless, shall thy lord
    Be by wanton base caress'd,
Nor, allured to other arms,
Wish, for venal beauty's charms,
    To leave thy tender breast.

He, as clasps the slender vine
  Trees that flourish by its side,
Shall be clasp'd in thy embrace;
But the daylight pales apace:
  Come forth! come forth, young bride!

. . . . .
. . . . .
. . . . .
. . . O!
Too radiant-footed bed!

What rich joys thy lord await,
  What rich joys in still night-tide,
What rich joys at noon of day;
But the daylight dies away:
  Come forth! come forth, young bride!

Youths! the flambeaux brandish high,
  See the saffron vèil's bright glow,
Sing in measure, swell the lay:
Hymen! Hymen! come, we pray,
  O Hymen! Hymen, O!

All around let now resound
  Songs of mirth and wanton glee;
Sharer of his former joys,
Shower among the happy boys
  The nuts they crave from thee.

Shower the nuts among the boys;
   Long enough 'twas thine to live
Sportive, and with nuts to play:
Manlius claims his bride to-day,
   The nuts then freely give.

Thou didst scorn the rustic throng
   But to-day and yesterday:
Loveliest leaves are soonest sere;
Youth is fleeting, age is near:
   Come, throw the nuts away.

Perfumed bridegroom! though thou griev'st,
   Bid thy cherish'd darling go,
Though thy heart be still as fain,
From the sports of youth abstain:
   O Hymen! Hymen, O!

Thou hast only join'd in those,
   By our laws allow'd, we know;
But what fits the youthful heart
Is not aye the husband's part:
   O Hymen! Hymen, O!

Never, youthful bride! deny
   What thou to thy lord dost owe,
Lest some freer girl decoy
Him with dreams of lawless joy:
   O Hymen! Hymen, O!

Lo! a rich and happy home
  Doth thy lord on thee bestow,
To be aye by thee possess'd,
(Hymenaeus! god thrice blest!
  O Hymen! Hymen, O!)

Even till feeble palsied age,
  Crown'd with locks of driven snow,
Listless lists to every call,
Witless nodding all to all:
  O Hymen! Hymen, O!

O'er the step with omen fair
  Lift her feet of golden glow:
Enter now the polish'd door:
Hymen, Hymen, evermore!
  O Hymen! Hymen, O!

See! thy husband lieth now
  On his Tyrian couch, and, lo!
Yearneth heart and soul for thee;
Come, O Hymen, fond and free!
  O Hymen! Hymen, O!

In his heart not less than thine
  Doth the flame of passion glow,
But a fiercer inward fire
Fills his soul with deep desire:
  O Hymen! Hymen, O!

Purple-mantled youth! now leave—
  Leave the maiden's arm of snow.
Let her to his couch repair,
Hymen, ever fond and fair!
  O Hymen! Hymen, O!

Matrons! who have faithful been
  To your faithful husbands, go,
Place the tender maid aright,
Place the maid with omen bright:
  O Hymen! Hymen, O!

Bridegroom! come! Thy radiant bride,
  With a rosy blush imbued,
In her chamber waits for thee,
Like a white parthenicè,
  Or poppy saffron-hued.

Husband! by the gods above!
  But thou none the less art fair,
Nor doth Venus thee despise;
But the daylight pales: arise,
  Nor linger longer there.

Neither hast thou linger'd long.
  Now thou 'rt come: may Venus prove
Favouring, since before our face
Thou thy darling dost embrace,
  And hid'st not virtuous love.

Of thy many thousand joys
  Who to tell the sum aspires,
May he sooner count the sands
On the Erythrēan strands,
  Or midnight's twinkling fires.

Sport at pleasure, and may soon
  Sons on sons up round you spring :
Let not such an ancient name
Wither in a childless fame,
  But aye be blossoming.

May a young Torquatus soon
  From his mother's bosom slip
Forth his tender hands, and smile
Sweetly on his sire the while,
  With half-oped tiny lip.

May each one a Manlius
  In his infant features see,
And may every stranger trace,
Clearly graven on his face,
  His mother's chastity.

May such praise, O blooming bride !
  Crown thy happy progeny,
As Telemachus retains,
Fruit of that best mother's veins,
  The chaste Penelope.

Virgins! now the portals close:
Cease your revels: now 'tis time,
Happy pair! to seal love's pledge;
Exercise your privilege
In youth's fond lusty prime.

LXII.

NUPTIAL SONG.

YOUTHS.

HESPERUS comes! ho, youths, arise! above Olympus'
    height
The star of eve at length displays his long-expected
    light:
'Tis time to rise—to leave the festal banquet, come
    away!
Soon will the virgin come, and soon be sung the bridal
    lay.
    Hymen, O Hymenaee! Hymen ades, O Hymenaee!

MAIDENS.

Ho, maidens! do ye see the youths? meet them with
    right goodwill,
Surely the Herald of the Night beams clear o'er Oeta's
    hill;

'Tis so: and see ye not how nimbly trip the youths along?
Nor leap'd they forth for nought: 'twere fame to conquer them in song.
   Hymen, O Hymenaee! Hymen ades, O Hymenaee!

YOUTHS.

Not easily, O youths! shall we the wreath of victory gain,
Mark how our fair-cheek'd rivals muse apart, nor muse in vain;
Right memorable is the lay the maidens have design'd;
Nor strange: since thus they ply their task with undivided mind.
With busy ears for bootless talk we've fritter'd time away,
A just defeat will then be ours: for labour gains the day;
Wherefore, let now at least the theme your careful study claim;
Hark! 'tis your rivals, now prepare responses meet to frame.
   Hymen, O Hymenaee! Hymen ades, O Hymenaee!

MAIDENS.

Hesper! what heaven-revolving orb beams with more cruel ray,
Who from the mother's arms the clinging child canst tear away,

NUPTIAL SONG.

And on the passion-burning youth the guileless girl
    bestow,
What deed more ruthless stains the town that's taken
    by the foe?
    Hymen, O Hymenaee! Hymen ades, O Hymenaee!

YOUTHS.

Hesper! what star with gladder radiance beams in
    yonder sky?
Who with thy flame the plighted nuptial vow dost
    ratify;
The sire's and suitor's pledge to seal thy beams alone
    have power:
What by the gods to mortals given can match this
    blissful hour?
    Hymen, O Hymenaee! Hymen ades, O Hymenaee!

MAIDENS.

Companions! Hesper from our midst has borne a
    white-robed mate:
Thou star of ill! whene'er thou com'st the watchers
    guard the gate,
The prowler lurks by night, and oft, in morning's
    shadows gray,
Thou, changed to Phosphor, lightest up the unhal-
    low'd spoiler's way.
    Hymen, O Hymenaee! Hymen ades, O Hymenaee!

YOUTHS.

To chide thee with feign'd railleries the maidens never tire,
What if they chide, while they with inmost soul thy beams desire?
  Hymen, O Hymenaee! Hymen ades, O Hymenaee!

MAIDENS.

As springs the sweet secluded flower in garden's fencèd space,
Unknown to browsing flock, untouch'd by ploughshare's grazing trace,
By breezes soothed, by sunshine fired, and foster'd by the rain,
Which many a youth and many a maiden fondly seek in vain;
When once nail-nipp'd, the faded flower, no youths, no maidens prize:
So, while the maid's a maid, she glads her friends' and playmates' eyes;
But when her sullied form has lost the virgin charms she wore,
To lover she's no longer dear, nor dear to maiden more.
  Hymen, O Hymenaee! Hymen ades, O Hymenaee!

YOUTHS.

As grows the unwedded vine within the bare and barren field,
Nor ever rears its head erect, nor mellow grape doth yield,

But, bending 'neath its weary weight, its sprays and
    roots entwined,
Withers and dies unheeded all by peasant or by
    hind :
When once elm-wedded, then by hind's and peasant's
    toil 'tis rear'd:
So, while the maid's a maid, she spends a lonely age
    uncheer'd,
But meetly wedded, in the golden springtide of
    desire,
She glads a loving husband's heart, nor grieves a
    doting sire.
    Hymen, O Hymenaee! Hymen ades, O Hymenaee!

YOUTHS AND MAIDENS.

Since such a husband shall be thine, O maiden ! come
    away !
He is thy sire's and mother's choice, whom thou
    must needs obey:
Thy sole disposal is not thine—a part thy parents
    claim—
Thy sire and mother each a third, to thee belongs
    the same :
'Twere unbeseeming to resist thy parents' double
    power,
Who to the bridegroom yield their rights, together
    with thy dower.
    Hymen, O Hymenaee! Hymen ades, O Hymenaee!

LXIII.

ATYS.

In eager haste in rapid bark young Atys cross'd the
 ˙billowy main,
Swift leap'd ashore, rush'd to the Phrygian grove,
 Cybebe's dark domain ;
And, goaded on by raging madness, frenzied inspira-
 tion's prey,
There, with a sharp-edged flinty stone, all trace of
 manhood swept away.

And when the sexless being saw the mutilated form
 he wore,
And gazed upon the ground bespatter'd with the warm
 and reeking gore,
Up in his snowy hand he caught the timbrel light,
 with furious glee,
The timbrel of thy dread initiate rites, great Mother
 Cybele!
And, rattling with his tender fingers on the bullock's
 hollow hide,
In accents wild and tremulous he thus to his com-
 panions cried:

"Away, ye Galli! hence! away to Cybele's high
    forests fly,
Away, ye roving crew! your mistress Dindymene's
    service ply,
Ye! who like exiles from your homes have sought
    strange lands, led on by me,
Who've dared the rapid briny deep, the raging fury
    of the sea,
And, loathing woman's charms, unmann'd your lusty
    forms with maiming rite,
On in your rapid wanderings speed, your souls with
    frenzy's fire incite!

"Drive from your minds all coward fears; haste,
    hither haste, and follow me!
On to your mistress' Phrygian shrine—the Phrygian
    groves of Cybele—
Where echoing cymbals clash, where timbrels roll
    around their swelling tone,
Where the Phrygian flutist's curvèd reed drones out
    its dreary moan,
Where raving Maenads madly toss their ivy-circled
    heads about,
And urge their hallow'd mysteries with shrieking yell
    and piercing shout,
Where to and fro the wandering crew of votaries de-
    light to stray,—
'Tis there, with wild careering, we must speed: away!
    away! away!"

When Atys, man no more, had thus unto his sexless
  comrades sung,
Suddenly the chorus raised the yell with frenzy-quiver-
  ing tongue,
Booms the light timbrel once again—again the hollow
  cymbals clash ;
On to green Ida with impetuous steps the frantic
  votaries dash.
Infuriate, panting, wild, bewilder'd, Atys, leading on
  the throng,
Smote the round timbrel's airy form, through murky
  forests rush'd along,
Like wild, unbroken heifer, bursting from the galling
  yoke, he fled,
The rapid Galli close behind their rapid-footed leader
  sped.

And when they, weak and wearied, reach their mistress Dindymene's home,
Fasting, they sink to sleep, their bodies with unmeas-
  ured toil o'ercome :
Dull languors o'er them steal, with heavy drowsiness
  their eyelids close :
And the raving madness of their souls is lull'd a while
  in calm repose.

But when the golden-visaged Orb of Day with eyes all
  radiant smiled
Upon the pale-hued sky of dawn, the solid earth, and
  ocean wild,

And with his thunder-footed steeds urged on the shades
 of night apace,
Then Sleep from Atys fled, and, trembling, sought
 Pasithea's embrace.

When now with sweet refreshing rest his furious
 frenzy was allay'd,
And Atys with untroubled soul his deeds in sober
 reason weigh'd,
And with unclouded mind beheld the sexless wretch
 he was, and where,
Back to the sea he rush'd, soul-toss'd upon the billows of despair,
And, gazing with tear-welling eyes upon the ocean's
 vast expanse,
Pour'd forth unto his native land this plaint, his woe's
 wild utterance:

" My country! land that gave me birth! from which,
 wretch that I am! I fled,
Like hireling from his master's roof, and to the groves
 of Ida sped,
There amid snows and frozen dens of savage brutes
 my lot to bear,
And rove, a frantic wretch, and rouse the forest prowler
 from his lair:

G

"Where shall I deem thee, parent clime? Oh! in
    what region dost thou lie?
While reason's fitful gleam remains, thee-ward I long
    to turn mine eye.
Must I now tread these dreary deserts, far, far distant
    from my home?
Far from my fatherland, possessions, friends, and
    parents, must I roam?
Banish'd the Forum, Race-course, Ring, debarr'd the
    loved Gymnasium's pale?
My wretched, wretched soul, for ever and for ever
    pour thy wail.

"What form is there I have not worn?—boy, youth,
    man, votaress?—on the soil
Of the Gymnasium I was first,—the pride and glory
    of the oil;
My gates were throng'd, my threshold warm, my home
    with flowery chaplets hung,
When morning woke me, and the sun his golden
    radiance o'er me flung.

"And must I serve the gods? alas! a howling slave
    of Cybele!
A Maenad! part of what I was,—a sterile, sexless
    devotee?

And must I ever on the snow-clad regions of green
    Ida pine,
And linger on 'neath Phrygia's frowning peaks while
    weary life is mine,
Where roams the woodland-nurtured stag, where
    prowls the forest-ranging boar?
Oh, now I rue the deed I've done, and mourn my
    rashness o'er and o'er."

When fell these accents from his rosy lips upon the
    wandering air,
The ears of the immortals caught the tidings of his
    wild despair;
Then Cybele unyoked her car, and freed the lions
    from her hold,
And, fiercely goading, thus harangued the left hand
    smiter of the fold:

"On, Savage! blast him with despair! on, on! in
    terror and dismay
Scare into yonder shaggy shades the caitiff wretch
    who'd flee my sway,
Go! sweep thy tail and lash thy flanks, roar till the
    forest roars again,
And wildly, fiercely toss upon thy brawny neck thy
    tawny mane."

Thus spake the awful Cybele, and freed her lion from
    the yoke.
Rousing his soul of fire, he rush'd, roar'd, through
    the crashing branches broke,
And when he near'd the lonely beach, white with the
    foam of ocean's tide,
And by the glassy mirror of the sea the tender Atys
    spied,
On with a bound he sprung. Back to his wilds the
    frantic being fled,
And there, 'mid dreary wastes, a life of servile bondage
    ever led.

O great and potent deity! O goddess dread and
    marvellous!
O Cybele divine! queen of the forest realms of Din-
    dymus,
From me and from my home thy inspirations wild be
    far away:
To thy dark rites and frenzied dreams be other votaries
    a prey!

LXIV.

THE NUPTIALS OF PELEUS AND THETIS.

'Tis said that pines that grew of yore on Pelion's
  woody height,
Sail'd far across the liquid realm that owns old Nep-
  tune's might,
Even to the waves of Phasis' stream and the Aeetæan
  strand:
When chosen youths—the beauty and the strength of
  Graecia's land—
With eager hearts to wrest from Colchian's hand the
  fleece of gold,
Sped through the briny deep, in rapid ship, their
  journey bold,
And dared with pliant oars of fir the plains of azure
  scour:
For these the goddess, who keeps ward in high em-
  battled tower,
A wheelless chariot form'd, to flit before the gentle
  breeze,
By fitting to a curvèd keel the closely-knitted trees.
That gallant bark first skimm'd along the erst unfur-
  row'd seas.

Soon as with forward prow the windy sea she cut in
    twain,
And the oar-tortured wave grew white with spray amid
    the main,
From out the seething gulf emerged, their faces wan
    with fright,
Sea Neréids, wrapt in wonder at the strange, un-
    wonted sight.
On that, and ne'er on other morn did mortal eyes
    behold
The ocean Nymphs unveil their forms of fair, immortal
    mould;
Up from their hoary home they rose, breast-low the
    wave above,
Then Peleus' soul, with Thetis fired, was kindled into
    love;
Then Thetis on a mortal's love look'd down with no
    disdain;
Then, too, her sire his sanction gave to the union of
    the twain.

Hail! race of heroes! Hail! whom birth an age far
    happier gave,
Hail! offspring of immortals! hail! blest mother of
    the brave!
And while I sing this lay of mine, I'll oft invoke
    your name;
Thine, too, whom such high nuptials crown with never-
    dying fame,

O Peleus! prop of Thessaly! to whom eternal Jove,
The almighty father of the gods, resign'd his cherish'd love.
Did Thetis, Nereus' fairest child, accept thy proffer'd hand?
Thy claim to wed their grandchild did old Tethys not withstand,
And Ocean who with welling waves encircles every land?

Soon as the rolling wheels of time brought round the long'd-for day,
To Peleus' home Thessalia's nobles flock without delay,
And crowds all joyous, wishing joy, thick throng the regal hall,
And many a present bring: joy beams upon the face of all.
Now Scyros' isle is left behind, and Phthian Tempe's homes,
And Crannon's dwellings, and Larissa's walls and stately domes,
All to Pharsalia hie; Pharsalia's halls in crowds they seek.
No peasant tills the fields, the bullock's neck grows soft and sleek,
The lowly vine no more is clear'd of weeds by crookèd rakes,
No more the bull with ploughshare prone the crumbling glebe upbreaks,

The pruner's hook no longer lops the trees' umbrageous boughs,
The squalid and corroding rust o'erspreads the unheeded ploughs.

But in the royal mansion, look around where'er you will,
The silver bright and shining gold your eyes with wonder fill;
On seats the polish'd ivory shines, on boards the goblets gleam,
And all the gorgeous palace-halls with regal splendours teem.
A couch in central chamber stood, whereon the bride might lie,
Inlaid with polish'd Indian tooth, and veil'd from vulgar eye
By coverlet of purple hue—the sea-shell's rosy dye;
And on this coverlet were wrought the forms of men of old,
Of heroes gone, whose high renown with wondrous art was told.

There Ariadne stood, on Dia's wave-resounding shore,
And wild o'ermastering agonies her gentle bosom tore;
Her gaze is fix'd on Theseus, as in rapid bark he flies,
Nor can she yet believe she sees the scene before her eyes—

That, on uprising from her bed, deceitful slumber
  gone,
She finds her wretched self upon the lonely sands
  alone.

But he, ungrateful youth! speeds fast his course with
  smiting oar,
His promise to the winds he throws, remembering it
  no more ;
On him, far from the weedy strand, she strains her
  sorrowing eyes,
A Bacchant's marble image, yelling forth her maddening cries :
Within her soul, like billows, roll the heaving waves
  of care,
Upon her brow no fillet now confines her golden
  hair,
No more with its light vesture is her snowy bosom
  wound,
No more the fine-wrought girdle binds her struggling
  breast around.
From all her body gliding down on every side they fall,
The salt sea-waves before her feet are sporting with
  them all.

She cares not for her floating veil, she cares not for
  her crown ;
What wonder if her lover's loss all other losses
  drown ?

Her heart, her soul, her mind by love's wild passions
  are consumed.
Ah! wretched Ariadne! to distracting sorrows doom'd!
For Venus many a thorny care implanted in thy mind,
What time heroic Theseus, leaving Athens' shores
  behind,
Did from Piraeus' winding coast his gallant vessel
  bring,
And enter the Gortynian halls of Crete's unrighteous
  king.

To wash away a direful plague—so ancient legends
  tell—
That for Androgeos' murder foul on Cecrops' city fell,
Her chosen youths and spotless maids were wont to
  sail afar
To Creta's isle—a banquet for the savage Minotaur:
And since the infant city groan'd beneath such
  grievous woes,
To give his life for his dear land brave Theseus rather
  chose
Than that Cecropia's youths should find, across the
  Cretan wave,
A funeral 'reft of funeral rites, within a living grave.

So, speeding in his rapid bark, borne on by gentle
  gales,
He reaches haughty Minos' realms, his regal palace
  hails.

Soon as the royal virgin's eager eye beholds his face—
The maid, who knows no other's, save a mother's fond embrace,
Round whose chaste bed sweet perfumes all their balmiest odours fling,
Fair as along Eurotas' banks the budding myrtles spring,
Or as the lovely flowers that streak spring's rainbow-colour'd wing—
She burns, nor ever turns away her passion-drunken eyes,
Till all amain through every vein love's flame enkindled flies,
And in her inmost marrow all its maddening frenzies rise.

O cruel maddener of the mind! divine, relentless boy!
Who ever minglest bitter grief with mortals' sweetest joy;
And thou, O queen of Golgos and Idalia's leafy glade,
On what a billowy sea ye toss'd that soul-enkindled maid!
What heavings for her fair-hair'd guest within her bosom roll'd!
What fears within her fainting heart made youth's warm blood run cold!
How oft more wan her cheek became than sheen of yellow gold!

And when he yearn'd to brave the savage monster in
    his lair,
And perish in his jaws, or earn the hero's guerdon
    there,
She vow'd heaven-pleasing offerings, to her how fruit-
    less now!
Nor linger'd on her silent lip in vain the unspoken
    vow.

For as the furious whirlwind, in its wild and eddying
    flight,
Uptears the oak that waves its boughs on Taurus'
    lofty height,
Or oozy cone-producing pine, with trunk of giant
    might:
Far from its roots upborne it headlong falls with
    furious bound,
Scattering, amid its crushing crash, destruction all
    around:
So, Theseus with victorious arm the savage monster
    slew,
That to the empty air his horns in vain uptossing
    threw.

Back, then, from forth the drear abyss with well-
    earn'd fame he sped,
Guiding his wandering footsteps with a skein of slen-
    der thread,

That he might keep his memory clear amid its winding ways,
And find a place of egress from the labyrinthine maze.

But why in this my song should more digressions find
   a place,
Why tell how Ariadne, having fled her father's face—
Fled a dear sister's loving arms, a mother's tender
   care,
A mother who bewail'd her child in accents of despair,
Her Theseus' honey'd love preferr'd all other things
   before,
Or how the ship was wafted on to Dia's foaming
   shore,
How then her husband, hard of heart, to every feeling
   steel'd,
Departing, left her, soon as fatal sleep her eyelids
   seal'd;
And oft, 'tis said, her passion-kindled soul with fury
   flush'd,
The piercing shrieks of rage from out her inmost
   bosom gush'd;
And now, that full of woe, she clomb the mountain's
   rugged steep,
Whence she could see outspread below the wide and
   swelling deep,
Anon the soft dress lifting that around her beauty
   hung,
She, rushing forward, laved her limbs the rippling
   waves among,

And there, with streaming eyes and uttering sobbings
    cold and faint,
The anguish'd maiden in her woe pour'd forth this
    wild complaint :

"And is it thus, false Theseus! far, far from her
    native land,
Thou leavest Ariadne on a lone and barren strand?
And dost thou, thus departing, heaven's high behests
    despise?
Ingrate, and carry home with thee thy cursèd per-
    juries !

"Could nothing change the purposes of thy unpitying
    mind?
Could no warm stream of mercy to thy soul a channel
    find?
Could thy relentless heart no pang of pity feel for
    me?
Ah! these are not the promises once fondly vow'd
    by thee ;
And these are not the joys my wretched hope was
    taught to prove,
But happy union and the long'd-for sweets of wedded
    love :
All scatter'd now, and strewn to every wind that
    sweeps the air.

" Henceforth let never woman trust an oath that man
    shall swear,
Nor count the tender speeches true his lying lips de-
    clare ;
For when with lusting soul he yearns some object to
    enjoy,
No oath, no promise then he deems too sacred to
    employ;
But when his soul is sated, and his burning passion
    dies,
He fears to break no plighted vows, cares nought for
    perjuries.

" 'Twas I who snatch'd thee from the gulf wide-
    yawning to devour,
And rather chose to doom to death my brother
    Minotaur,
Than fail thee, thou deceitful one ! in danger's awful
    hour ;
For this to savage beasts and birds a prey shall I be
    thrown,
And no kind hand shall heap the dust on me when
    life is gone.

" What lioness gave birth to thee in lone rock-
    shelter'd cave ?
What sea conceived and spued thee forth from its
    wild foaming wave ?

Syrtis, or ravenous Scylla, or Charybdis vast and stern?
Who for sweet life by me preserved dost render such return.
And if to wed me now thy heart, all-changed, had no desire,
Because thou loath'dst the stringent laws of my relentless sire,
At least thou mightst have carried me to thy own native land,
That I with pleasant labour might have served at thy command,
With the water's limpid stream I would have laved
. thy snow-white feet,
Or gladly spread upon thy bed its purple coverlet.

" But wherefore, madden'd with my woes, should I thus, all in vain,
To the unconscious senseless air with wailings wild complain?
It cannot hear my utter'd words, nor answer make again:
For surely now his sails the ocean's midmost billows reach,
And not a human form is seen on this lone, weedy beach;
Thus in my latest hour, stern fate, insulting and severe,
From my unheeded, hopeless cry, averts her envious ear.

"Oh how I wish, Almighty Jove! that ne'er in days of yore
A ship from the Cecropian land had reach'd the Gnossian shore,
Nor, to the indomitable bull bearing his tribute dire,
The faithless mariner had sought the kingdom of my sire;
Nor, in sweet guise concealing the fell purpose of his breast,
That villain in my Cretan home had rested as a guest.
Ruin'd, alas! what hope is left? or whither shall I flee?
The mountains of Idomene?—the cruel, severing sea,
With its broad trackless gulf, divides that friendly land from me.
Can I expect a father's aid whose countenance I fled,
Following the stern-soul'd youth whose arm my brother's blood had shed?
Or from a husband's faithful love what solace can I reap?
Deserted he has left me, and his oars now ply the deep.
On this lone shore, this desert isle, no dwelling can be found,
No egress hence—the ocean rolls a barrier all around;
There are no means of flight; no hope; mute desolation reigns;
Death staring me on every side, my certain doom remains.

"Yet shall my languid eyes not cease to gaze upon
    the day,
Nor from my wearied body shall the senses ebb
    away,
Till on his head I beg the gods meet punishment to
    pour,
And, thus betray'd, in my last hour heaven's holy faith
    implore.

"Ye powers! who to the crimes of men dire chastise-
    ment assign;
Eumenides! around whose heads the snaky ringlets
    twine;
Whose brows portray the hellish wrath that rankles in
    your breast;
Oh! hither, hither haste, and list to this the sad re-
    quest
Which from my inmost soul, alas! to misery con-
    sign'd,
I'm forced to pour—a helpless wretch, with burning
    madness blind;
And since even from my bosom's depths these bursts
    of anguish stream,
Oh, doom them not to vanish like an airy, idle
    dream,
But let him in that soul, in which he has abandon'd
    me,
Bring on himself and all his race death and black
    infamy."

When, with sad heart, she pour'd this plaint, and, wild
    with woe, besought
Fierce retribution for the deeds of wrong that he had
    wrought,
Her prayer the King Celestial heard, and awful
    bow'd assent;
Earth and wild ocean trembled at his nod omnipo-
    tent,
And all the glittering worlds were rock'd in the vast
    firmament.

Then was the mind of Theseus with a darkening
    gloom opprest,
And every mandate that before his constant soul pos-
    sest
Was swept away, to rise no more in his forgetful
    breast:
Nor did he to his sorrowing sire the gladdening signs
    display
In token of his safe return to the Athenian bay.

For ere the fleet left Pallas' seat to plough the briny
    wave,
Ere Aegeus trusted yet his son the stormy winds to
    brave,
'Tis said he clasp'd him to his breast, and these in-
    junctions gave:

" My peerless boy! oh, dearer far to me than length of days,
Whom I am now compell'd to send in danger's dubious ways!
My son! but just restored to me in latest life's last stage,
Since my own evil fortune and thy valour's burning rage
Tear thee from my unwilling heart, ere yet my feeble eyes
Rest on thy lovèd form till time their craving satisfies:
I will not send thee from my face with gladden'd heart elate,
Nor suffer thee to bear away signs of propitious fate;
But first full many a bitter wail shall from my bosom flow,
And with the earth and sprinkled dust I'll soil my locks of snow,
Then, on thy flitting mast, dyed sails I'll hang aloft in air,
That with its dark Iberian hue thy canvas may declare
What burning anguish wrings my soul, what pangs my bosom tear.
And should the goddess, who in blest Itone has her shrine,
(The guardian of our native land, protectress of our line,)
Grant that the monster's blood be shed by strong right arm of thine,

'Then see that in thy memory stored these precepts still have weight,
Nor lapse of time e'er from thy mind my words obliterate,
And when thy native hills again shall rise before thine eye,
Let everywhere thy sail-yards drop their robes of dismal dye,
And let the twisted ropes the snow-white canvas hoist on high,
That when I see it my glad heart glad tidings there may trace,
When that auspicious day restores thee to thy father's face."

These mandates, that before he kept close treasured in his mind,
Fled from his darken'd memory, nor left a trace behind,
Like cloud from snow-capt mountain's crest swept by a gale of wind.

His sire, as from a turret's top he scann'd the ocean's rim,
His anxious eyes with ever-flowing tears fast waxing dim,

When the dark canvas of the inflated sail first hove in
    sight,
Believing Theseus lost by cruel death's relentless
    might,
Dash'd forward with a headlong bound from the dim
    craggy height.

Thus Theseus, when he reach'd his home, which
    death's dark woes opprest,
Was in his heart by such soul-agonising griefs dis-
    trest,
As his ingratitude had fix'd in Ariadne's breast,
When, anguish-wrung, she traced the ship receding
    from her view,
And in her breast roll'd countless woes in aspect ever
    new.

Elsewhere " Iacchus, ever young," flies hurrying from
    above,
Round whom the Satyrs and the Nysa-rear'd Sileni
    rove,
O Ariadne, seeking thee, and, fired with frantic love :
See how with frenzied souls they rave, with fleet foot
    speeding by,
And " Evöe, Evöe," wildly shout, and toss their heads
    awry ;
Some brandish in their hands aloft the ivy-circled
    spear,
Some hurl about the mangled limbs of a dismember'd
    steer,

Some all around their naked forms the wriggling serpents plait,
Some with their wicker-basket stores dark orgies celebrate,
Orgies for ever seal'd except to ears initiate:
There, with extended palms, some smite the timbrel's airy round,
Or from the polish'd brazen plates wake the shrill tinkling sound;
By many, too, the trumpet's hoarsely-sounding blare is blown,
And the barbaric pipe creaks forth its wild, ear-piercing tone.

With forms like these the coverlet, all gorgeously bespread,
Enfolded with its drapery and veil'd the bridal bed.
Fill'd with the scenes that with delight their eager spirits fired,
Ere yet the holy gods approach'd Thessalia's youths retired.
As Zephyr crisps, with early breath, the still and sleeping sea,
What time around the wandering Sun Dawn bids the shadows flee,
And wakes the sloping waves to life and morning liberty;
While, by a gentle breeze first fann'd, they undulating flow,
And with a rippling murmur utter laughter soft and low;

Then, when the freshening gale blows strong, wild and more wildly war,
And, flowing from the purple dawn, refulgent gleam afar:
So from the royal vestibule slow pour'd the crowds away,
Then homeward sped with quickening tread each as his journey lay.

The crowd now gone, from Pelion's height old Chiron first appear'd,
Bearing for nuptial offerings what stores the country rear'd,
For flowers of every hue that o'er Thessalia's meadows grow,
That stud her giant mountain-slopes or by her rivers blow,
Drawn from the pregnant earth by warm Favonius' fostering glow,
A rustic gift he brought, in plaited garlands, random-wreathed,
And all the palace wore a smile, and fragrant odours breathed.

Forthwith Peneus came, from Tempe's vale with verdure crown'd,
Tempe, which dark o'erhanging forest pine-trees mantle round,

Now left for Dorian dances of the beauteous Naiad
    throng;
Nor came he empty-handed—root and stem he bore
    along
The lofty beeches and the stately laurel's tapering
    trees,
The airy cypress, and the plane that flaunteth in the
    breeze,
And thunder-blasted Phäethon's tall sister; all of
    these
He placed around the mansion, laced the boughs the
    trunks between,
That all the vestibule might wear a robe of leafy
    green.

Behind him next Prometheus came, deep-versed in
    cunning lore,
Still wearing feeble traces of the punishment he
    bore
When from the barren jagged flinty crags that o'er
    him frown'd,
Erewhile he hung, his limbs with adamantine shackles
    bound.

Then Jove himself, his holy spouse, and all his progeny,
Came from the heavenly mansion, leaving, Phoebus,
    only thee,
And thy twin-sister, who delights on Idrus' hill to be :

For, like thee, thy fair sister nursed 'gainst Peleus
    bitter spite,
Nor with her presence deign'd to honour Thetis' nup-
    tial rite.

When on the seats the immortals bent their snowy
    limbs around
A board with viands manifold and choicest dainties
    crown'd,
Then, while all through their feeble frames the palsied
    tremors ran,
The Ancient Fates their truth-predicting canticle be-
    gan.
Their trembling forms on every side a mantling vest-
    ment veil'd
Of stainless white, around their heels its purple border
    trail'd;
On their ambrosial heads sat wreaths that with the
    snow had vied,
While their untiring hands their endless labour cease-
    less plied.
Their left hand held the distaff, shrouded in the wool's
    soft bed,
The right, with upturn'd fingers, gently drew and
    form'd the thread,
Then twisting it upon the thumb that pointed to the
    ground,
Kept the well-balanced spindle ever smoothly whirling
    round:

With nipping tooth they smoothed the work where'er
  a tuft appear'd,
And ever to their parchèd lips the woolly scraps adhered,
Which from the fine-spun thread with constant care
  they clear'd away.
Before their feet the shining wool in soft white fleeces
  lay
In baskets wrought with willow-wands, all scrupulously
  stored;
And as they drew the fleeces forth the prescient sisters
  pour'd,
With voices shrill, in strains divine, this song of destiny,
A song whose truth no after age will question or deny:

" Peleus! thou brilliant ornament! thou valour-
  crownèd one!
Great bulwark of Emathia's land! most glorious in
  thy son,
Hear, in this joyous hour, thy true, thy changeless
  future read;
Then, spindles, twine the threads by which dark destiny is sped,
Run, spindles! onward! spindles, run, and twine the
  fatal thread.

" Soon, soon shall Hesper come to crown thy fond
  marital dreams,
And lead to thee thy beauteous bride with happy-
  omen'd beams,

Thy bride, who in soul-trancing bliss thy panting soul
    shall steep,
And love-o'erwearied sink with thee in balmy languid
    sleep,
While all around thy manly neck her ivory arm she'll
    spread.
Run, spindles! ever ceaseless run, and twine the fatal
    thread.

"No house hath ever witness been to love so blest
    as this,
No love hath ever lovers join'd in such dear bond of
    bliss
As now awaits this happy pair, this happy nuptial
    bed.
Run, spindles! ever ceaseless run, and twine the fatal
    thread.

"To you Achilles shall be born, a hero void of
    fear,
His back to foe he'll never show, but breast un-
    daunted rear,
And when oft in the devious course the victor's path
    he'll tread,
The fleet stag's lightning footsteps shall by him be far
    outsped.
Run, spindles! ever ceaseless run, and twine the fatal
    thread.

" Though valiant heroes seek the field no equal shall
  he know,
When with the noblest blood of Troy the Phrygian
  plains will flow,
And the third heir of perjured Pelops devastation
  dread
In that long weary siege shall round the Trojan bul-
  warks spread.
Run, spindles! ever ceaseless run, and twine the fatal
  thread.

" To all his gifts heroic, to all his deeds of fame,
Mothers shall bear their witness beside the funeral
  flame,
When in the dust their hoary hairs they'll loosen from
  their head,
And feebly smite their aged breasts in anguish for the
  dead.
Run, spindles! ever ceaseless run, and twine the fatal
  thread.

" For as the reaper moweth down the unnumber'd
  ears of grain
When crops 'neath autumn's burning sun wave yellow
  o'er the plain,
So in the field he'll reap the Trojan foe with hostile
  blade.
Run, spindles! ever ceaseless run, and twine the fatal
  thread.

"A witness to his valiant deeds Scamander's flood
    shall be,
Which, sparsely streaming to the rapid Hellespontic
    sea,
Shall roll his dark corse-cumber'd waves pent in a
    narrower bed,
A warm ensanguined river, rolling billows crimson-red.
Run, spindles! ever ceaseless run, and twine the fatal
    thread.

"A witness, too, shall be the death-deliver'd captive
    maid,
When on the lofty earth-raised mound her snow-white
    limbs are laid
Prostrate beneath the axe's stroke—an offering to the
    dead.
Run, spindles! ever ceaseless run, and twine the fatal
    thread.

"For when to the war-wearied Greeks the Fates shall
    grant at length
To crush the walls by Neptune rear'd, the Dardan
    city's strength,
Polyxena, like victim stooping to the two-edged steel
On bended knee, a mangled, headless corse shall for-
    ward reel,
And on the hero's lofty tomb the appeasing stream
    shall shed.
Run, spindles! ever ceaseless run, and twine the fatal
    thread.

" Come, then, in wedlock's blissful bonds your loving hearts unite,
Now let the bridegroom take his goddess-bride with omen bright,
Now let the vestal to her husband's eager arms be led.
Run, spindles! ever ceaseless run, and twine the fatal thread.

" Her nurse, when morning streaks the sky with blushes rosy-red,
Shall find the necklace all too strait she wore when she was wed.
Run, spindles! ever ceaseless run, and twine the fatal thread.

" Nor shall her anxious mother mourn a separated bed,
But children's children shall arise before her hopes are fled.
Run, spindles! ever ceaseless run, and twine the fatal thread."

Such were the fates of Peleus, such the oracles benign,
The prescient sisters hymn'd in days of yore, with voice divine ;

For erst the heavenly gods appear'd in hero's chaste
   abode,
And 'mid assembled throngs of men their holy presence show'd;
While Piety, still undespised, maintain'd her saintly
   reign.
Oft then the Father of the gods re-sought his fulgent
   fane,
What time his annual sacred rites on festal days came
   round,
And saw a hundred slaughter'd bulls fall welt'ring to
   the ground.

Oft from Parnassus' lofty brow the roving Bacchus
   flew,
And drove along his hair-dishevell'd, yelling Thyad
   crew,
While from the city's every nook the Delphians rush'd
   abroad,
And at their smoking altars hail'd with joy the rosy
   god.

Oft to the deadly strife of war great Mars in armour
   sped,
Or rapid Triton's goddess-queen, or Rhamnus' maiden
   dread,
And, rousing mortals to the charge, the armèd legions
   led.

But when in awful wickedness the earth deep-stainèd lay,
And mortals from their lustful souls fair Justice chased away,
When brother in a brother's blood his murderous hands imbrued,
When son without a pang of grief his lifeless parents view'd;
When father fondly yearn'd that death might snatch his first-born boy,
That an unwedded step-dame's charms he freely might enjoy;
When mother, daring with her all-unconscious son to lie,
Fear'd not to stain her household gods in her impiety;
When right and wrong, in guilty madness mingled, met the view,
Their justice-loving minds from man the holy gods withdrew;
Wherefore for such assemblies now they never leave the sky,
Nor in unclouded day endure the gaze of mortal eye.

LXV.

TO HORTALUS.

Though ceaseless griefs and cares my heart devour,
    And call me from the learnèd Virgins' fane,
And though my woe-toss'd mind hath lost the power
    To breathe sweet poesy's melodious strain;

For o'er my brother's foot, clay-hued and chill,
    Flows Lethe's dark, inevitable wave;
And, ravish'd from my sight, his ashes fill,
    By far Rhoeteum's shore, a Trojan grave;

Though, Brother! I no more thy voice shall hear,
    Ne'er see thy life-dear face in after day,
Yet surely ever will I hold thee dear,
    And aye with grief's wan hues I'll tinge my lay;

Yea, even as the Daulian bird her song
    Outpours in accents sweetly dolorous,
When o'er the branch-gloom'd river all night long
    She wails the fate of perish'd Itylus:

Yet, Hortalus, in Latin garb I've drest
    For thee this poem of Battiades,
Lest thou shouldst think thy wish had fled my breast,
    A bootless offering to the roving breeze.

As glides the apple—furtive token fraught
   With tenderest love—from modest maiden's breast,
Who, with heart-deep emotions all distraught,
   Forgets the treasure 'neath her silken vest,

Which, when she springs her mother's kiss to claim,
   In all the innocence of girlish glee,
Slips out and rolls along, while conscious shame
   Crimsons her rueful face ;—*'twas so with me.*

LXVI.

BERONICE'S HAIR.

(Translated by Catullus from the Greek of Callimachus.)

CONON, who knew the great world's every light,
The rise and setting of the orbs of night,
How rapid Sol's bright beams eclipsed can die,
How stars at stated periods leave the sky,
How dulcet love to Latmos' rocks a while
From her aërial course did Trivia wile :
He saw me in the heavens new glory shed,
Me, the fair lock from Beronicè's head,
Which she to many a god in dread alarms
Had vow'd to give with outstretch'd ivory arms,

What time, in nuptial flush, her royal lord
Against Assyria sped with ruthless sword,
Wearing sweet scars from that nocturnal fray
In which he bore her virgin spoils away.

Do brides hate wedlock? or their parents' joy
With floods of lying tears would they destroy,
When o'er the nuptial chamber threshold led?
False, by the gods, are all the tears they shed!
Thou taught'st me this with many a sad lament,
When to grim wars, O Queen, thy husband went;
Yet a lorn couch alone thou didst not mourn,
No: but a brother from a sister torn.
What anguish then thy inmost marrow tore!
What cares thy bosom harrow'd to the core,
Reaving thy soul of sense! yet sure had I
Known thee from earliest years of courage high.
Hadst thou forgot the deed that crown'd thee queen,
Than which fame's roll no braver boasts, I ween?
Yet when he left thee, O ye gods! what sighs!
How oft thy wan hands wiped thy streaming eyes!
What god thee changed? or will not lovers dwell
Far from the ones they inly love so well?
'Twas then thou vowedst to all the gods to give
Me, with the blood of bulls, should he but live,
And, soon to thee returning, add in chains
The Asian land to Egypt's wide domains:
For these dear boons, in heaven's host number'd now,
With virgin beams I pay thy pristine vow.
O Queen! I left thy head unwillingly—
Unwillingly: yes, by thy head and thee!

Who slights this oath meet vengeance let him feel;
But who can dare oppose the might of steel?
By steel that mountain e'en was prostrate laid,
The greatest Thia's radiant son survey'd,
When Medan hosts a new sea form'd, and through
Mid Athos swept the fierce barbarian crew;
How shall poor tresses, then, fell steel dare face?
Great Jove! in ire blast all the Chalyb race,
And him who first the embowell'd treasures tore
From forth the earth, and steel'd the veinèd ore.

The sister locks I left still mourn'd my fate,
When Aethiop Memnon's brother, through heaven's gate
Rushing, with quivering wings the ether clove,
And to Arsinoë's shrine impetuous drove.
He took me up: up through heaven's gloom he prest,
And laid me down on Venus' spotless breast;
For Grecian Venus' self gave this command,
Hight Zephyritis on Canopus' strand,
That not alone, high in the star-gemm'd sky,
On Ariadne's brow should man descry
A golden crown, but that I too should shine,
Even I, the golden curl that graced her shrine.
She placed me here, still moist with many tears,
A new-made star among the primal spheres;
Close by the Virgin and the Lion wild,
To fierce Callisto near, Lycaon's child;
Westward I veer and slow Boötes guide,
That hardly sinks at last in ocean's tide;

Though down at night by feet immortal prest
Dawn calls me back to fair-hair'd Tethys' breast ;
Yet—let me speak it, dread Rhamnusian maid,
For I will speak the truth all undismay'd,
And though with kindling ire the stars should seethe,
The dictates of a truthful breast I'll breathe—
My lot so glads me not that I would be
Thus rack'd and ever barr'd, dear Queen, from thee,
With whom, a maid, I quaff'd no scents divine ;—
In wedlock ! gods ! what perfumes rare were mine.

Ye whom the long'd-for bridal-torch doth bind
To lords of loyal heart and kindred mind,
Yield not to them, nor all your charms display,
Till me sweet fee your onyx-boxes pay,
Ye who desire a husband's chaste caress ;
But let the gifts of foul adulteress,
Ah ! loathsome offerings ! slake the shifting sand,
No boon I crave from her unhallow'd hand.
So more and more, ye brides, may concord reign,
And love eternal in your homes remain.

And, Queen ! when to the stars thine eyes thou 'lt turn,
And, wooing Venus, festal torches burn,
Oh, be not me, thine own, from unguents free,
But dower me largely. Stars ! why hold ye me ?
Let me but grace once more that brow divine,
Orion then may next Aquarius shine.*

---

* Another rendering of the concluding lines of this poem, with special reference to the text of *Ellis*, will be found in the *Notes*.

LXVII.

DIALOGUE BETWEEN CATULLUS AND A DOOR.

(From the text of Rossbach.)

Catullus. HAIL, door! to husband and to parent dear,
And thee may Jove with every blessing cheer;
'Tis said thou servèdst Balbus well erewhile,
When that old man possess'd this domicile;
And that thou basely serv'dst his son again,
When with his bride the aged wight had lain;
Say, wherefore art thou deem'd so sadly changed,
And from thine ancient faith so far estranged?
    Door. No, (may it please Caecilius! whose I'm now,)
Though mine 'tis call'd, the fault's not mine, I trow,
Nor e'er could mortal tax me with a sin,
Though, sooth, the rabble make a hideous din,
· And when a fault's committed, all combine,
And shout at me: " Fie, door, the fault is thine."
    Catullus. Thy word alone is not enough for me;
Come, let me clearly understand and see.
    Door. How can I? no one asks or cares to know.
    Catullus. I do; speak on; away your scruples throw.

Door. First, then, 'tis said, she here a virgin
came;
'Tis false: not that her lord had been to blame,
For he, poor fellow, could not fail to prove
A harmless warrior in the lists of love;
But his old sire caress'd the blooming spouse,
And stain'd with infamy the ill-starr'd house;
Whether he burn'd with passion's lawless fire,
Or thought his sterile son must needs require
The help of one with stronger nerve and bone
To loose the new-made spouse's maiden zone.
 Catullus. You tell a noble parent's pious deed,
Good soul! to help his son in time of need.
 Door. But not of this alone does Brixia speak;
Brixia, that lies 'neath dark-blue* mountain peak,
Cleft by the yellow Mella's gentle wave,
Brixia, that birth to my Verona gave,
Tells of Posthumius' and Cornelius' fires
With whom she gratified her dark desires.
 Catullus. "Come, door, how know'st all this?"
some one may say,
"Thou from thine owner's threshold may'st not stray,
Nor hear the people talk, but night and day,
Fix'd to this post, must back or forward sway?"
 Door. Oft have I heard her tell, in furtive tone,
Her crimes, when with her maidens all alone,

---

* In the editions I have consulted, all the readings of this very obscure passage appear to me alike unsatisfactory. The second word of the line (32) is variously given, *Chinea*, *Chinaeae*, *Cenomanae*, *Echinaeae*, *Cygnea*, *Cycnea*, *Cycneae*, &c. I have conjectured *Cyaneae*.

Naming the aforesaid ones, as if I here
Kept swinging, gifted with nor tongue nor ear.
She mention'd one besides who'll nameless be,
Lest he with bristling eyebrows scowl on me—
A lean, lank fellow, once in law involved
About a case of birth he wanted solved.

LXVIII.*

EPISTLE TO MANLIUS.

Oppress'd with woe and misery's crushing gloom,
    You send to me a letter writ in tears,
Imploring help and rescue from the tomb,
    Like the wreck'd seaman who the wild waves fears;

To whom, on your lone, widow'd bed reclined,
    Nor holy Venus grants sweet rest by night,
Nor doth the Muse your rest-robb'd anguish'd mind
    With the sweet strains of ancient bards delight.

Your lines are dear, since there you call me friend,
    And ask the gifts of Friendship and the Muse;
But, lest you know not 'neath what woes I bend,
    Or think I could such sacred claims refuse;

O Manlius! learn the ills that round me press,
    Plunged in the waves of sorrow's surging sea,
Nor longer think the boons of happiness
    Can be obtain'd from hapless wretch like me.

What time the vestment pure was round me thrown,
    In youth's glad spring all redolent of flowers,
I sported freely; not to Her unknown
    Who blends sweet bitterness with cares of ours.

Such thoughts thy woe-worn friend no more employ,
    Reft of a brother dear in manhood's bloom;
Brother! thy death has marr'd my every joy,
    With thee our house's glory finds a tomb.

With thee has perish'd every dear delight,
    Which o'er my life thy love's sweet influence shed;
Thy death has merged my soul in rayless night,
    Each taste, each pleasure that I loved has fled.

Why write me then? "Catullus, 'tis a shame
    Your life should thus be in Verona led,
While any gallant here of noble name
    May warm his chill limbs in your vacant bed."

Manlius, 'tis not a shame: 'tis piteous, say;
    And pardon me, if thee I do not send
The gifts which grief from me has torn away;
    They are not mine, nor on my will depend.

Of writings here I have but scanty store—
   A few choice books to soothe my hours of care;
For Rome is still my home as heretofore,
   My dwelling-place—my thoughts—my all is there.

Then think not I have thy requests denied
   From disingenuous soul or spiteful spleen;
Amply I would have both thy wants supplied,
   Unask'd by thee, if mine the power had been.

LXVIII.[b]

TO ALLIUS.

YE Muses! I cannot the meed withhold
   From Allius, for his help and loving zeal;
May fleeting years, to dark oblivion roll'd,
   Ne'er in night's dreary gloom his worth conceal.

To you I sing. Do ye in after days
   To thousands yet unborn his name extol,
And let this writing herald forth his praise,
   When it is reckon'd as an ancient scroll.

And when he's number'd with the silent dead,
   More and more glorious be his growing fame,
Nor let the pendent spider ever spread
   Her airy web o'er his neglected name.

Ye know how wily Venus plagued my life,
  And with resistless passion thrill'd my frame,
When in my vitals warr'd the fiery strife,
  Fierce as Sicilian Aetna's scorching flame,

Or as the boiling Malian springs that rise
  Within Thermopylae, by Oeta's hill,
Grief's bitter tears ne'er ceased to blur mine eyes,
  Nor sorrow's stream adown my cheek to trill.

As crystal rill from mountain's airy crest
  Leaps from the mossy stone and valeward bounds,
Then cuts the busy road—refreshment blest
  To way-worn wight when cracks the sun-baked grounds:

And as to storm-toss'd sailor comes the fair
  And gentle breeze that calms the angry sea,
From Pollux now, now Castor sought in prayer,
  So great a boon has Allius been to me.

He gave me wider fields, a home, its queen—
  Our love—my radiant goddess thither bore
Her sandall'd fairy foot with graceful mien,
  And made sweet music on my household floor.

Thus warm Laodamia sought of old
  Protesiläus' home, ah! sought in vain,
For never there the sacred blood had roll'd,
  Of victim to the blest immortals slain.

TO ALLIUS.

May ne'er be mine, Rhamnusian maiden stern,
    While heaven denies, desires inordinate;
How thirstily for blood the altars yearn
    Laodamia learn'd, alas! too late.

Forced from her young lord's loving arms to part,
    Ere in their laggard nights two winters view'd
Love's brimming chalice sate her eager heart,
    That she might live in weary widowhood.

Well knew the fates that doom not distant far,
    If he in arms to Ilium's walls should go,
For Helen's rape had roused the trump of war,
    And call'd the Argive chiefs to face the foe.

Fell Ilium! Europe's, Asia's common tomb,
    Troy! cruel grave of all that's brave and true,
'Twas there my brother fell by ruthless doom,
    Whose loss I'm left in bitterness to rue.

Brother, thou 'rt gone; alas! life's gladsome light!
    With thee the glory of our house is dead;
With thee has perish'd every dear delight
    Which o'er my life thy love's sweet influence shed.

'Mong nameless graves thou liest, far away,
    Near kindred dust placed by no kindly hand;
But Troy, foul, baleful Troy, detains thy clay,
    Thy grave a foreign clime's remotest strand!

Thither then hastening, all the youth of Greece,
   From hearth and home, in crowds innumerous sped,
That Paris with his stolen quean in peace
   Might not enjoy a quiet bridal bed.

Thus wast thou reft, incomparable bride,
   Of what than life and soul was sweeter bliss,
Love's all-absorbing, wildly-eddying tide
   Had suck'd thee down a fathomless abyss,

Vast as by Cyllene Pheneus was the one
   That drain'd the fertile soil—a marsh before—
And which Amphitryon's falsely-father'd son
   Dug in the bowels of the hill of yore,

When he by meaner lord's behest had driven
   'Gainst the Stymphalian pests the shafts of doom,
That one god more might tread the courts of heaven,
   Nor Hebe linger long in maiden bloom.

Far deeper than that gulf thine own deep love,
   That taught thee, all untaught, the yoke to bear,
Nor e'er did aged grandsire's deeper prove
   When first he hail'd his long-expected heir,*

---

* Or, according to other texts:—
   But thy deep love exceeded far the abyss
      That taught a servile god the yoke to bear,
   Nor e'er had agèd grandsire equal bliss
      When first he hail'd his long-expected heir,

And blest his only daughter's late-born boy,
  Who, in his will recorded in their stead,
Blasting his baffled kinsmen's impious joy,
  Scares off the vultures from his hoary head.

Nor ever joy'd so in her snowy mate
  The dove, with billing blisses ne'er content,
Whose eager love, 'tis said, no joys can sate,
  Though for inconstancy pre-eminent.

Great are the loves of these, but nought beside
  Thy matchless love, Laodamia fair,
When thou in wedlock's bonds becam'st the bride
  Of thy dear husband of the golden hair.

In nought or little less in charms the maid,
  My love! my life! came bounding to my breast,
Round whom oft Cupid, hovering glory-ray'd,
  Effulgent shone, in saffron tunic drest.

And though she may not live for me alone,
  Few are the falsehoods of my modest maid;
Then let me bear them as to me unknown,
  Nor like a fool her broken faith parade.

Oft Juno, mightiest of the powers above,
  Burn'd for her lord, though daily slights she bare,
For well she knew the amours of roving Jove;
  But gods with men 'tis impious to compare.

Still let me ne'er her anxious parent dread,
  Nor to my ears his peevish grumblings come,
For not by father's right hand was she led
  Into my Syrian-odour-scented home :

But on that wondrous night the charms her lord
  Of right deserved, on me she lavish'd free ;
Enough : if she with whiter stone record
  The hours she consecrates to love and me.

Allius! for many kindnesses I give
  The best return I can, this friendly lay,
That with foul rust unstain'd thy name may live
  Upon my page for ever and for aye.

What gifts of old to Virtue Themis paid,
  With these a gracious heaven thy days will cheer,
Then blest be thou, and blest thy life-dear maid,
  Our home of pleasure and its mistress dear.

And blest be he who added to my life
  The gift of friendship, when he added thee ;
But yet more blest and dear my more than wife,
  Light of my eyes, whose love is life to me.

LXIX.

TO RUFUS.

Wonder not, Rufus, why no maiden fair
  Will have your love or let your arms come near her,
Not though you tempt her with a vestment rare,
  Or lovely gem than sparkling water clearer.

A certain ugly story damns your suit;
  A buck-goat lurks, 'tis said, your arm-pits under;
The girls all fear the horrid, grewsome brute—
  For so he is—and, really, 'tis no wonder.

No longer deem it strange they're cold and coy,
  For till he's gone not one will venture nigh you;
At once this shocking nasal pest destroy,
  Or cease to wonder why the maidens fly you.

———◆———

LXX.

ON THE INCONSTANCY OF WOMAN'S LOVE.

Lesbia declares she'd marry none but me,
Not even Jove, should he her wooer be;
She says so: but on wind and rapid wave
A woman's troth to her fond swain engrave.

K

LXXI.

TO VIRRO.

If e'er to worthy's lot befell
The grievance of a goatish smell;
If e'er poor mortal limp'd about
A martyr to the racking gout;
Your lucky rival, on my oath,
Has got a glorious share of both.
So, oft as with your love he's lain,
You've had your vengeance on the twain:
His odour well-nigh chokes the fair,
His gout is more than man can bear.

LXXII.

TO LESBIA.

O Lesbia! once thou didst declare
   Catullus only had thy love;
That thou his lot wouldst rather share
       Than win the heart of Jove.

How pure that love of mine the while!
   It was not like the vulgar fires
That kindle at the wanton's wile,
       But holy as a sire's.

I know thee now: and though I glow
  With passion wilder than before,
To me thou 'rt vile and fallen low,
    My soul's delight no more.

How can it be? thy faithless ways,
  So grievous in a lover's sight,
Make passion's torch more fiercely blaze,
    But dim love's holy light.

LXXIII.

ON AN INGRATE.

Oh! cease to wish from any one a kindly thought to merit,
Or yet to think you can inspire a meek and grateful spirit;
All are ungrateful; all, alas! kind deeds avail us nothing;
Nay, more, they rather weary, cloy, and lead to utter loathing;
For he in fierce and bitter hate to no sworn foe is second,
Who lately had in me the one, the only friend he reckon'd.

LXXIV.

ON GELLIUS.

Gellius had heard his uncle used to scold,
If he of wanton word or deed was told;
To save himself, he kiss'd his uncle's wife,
And render'd him Harpocrates for life.
He gain'd his point: for, do whate'er he may,
His uncle now has not a word to say.

LXXV.

TO LESBIA.

Lesbia! no woman e'er was loved
   As thou hast been by me;
No plighted troth has ever proved
   So true as mine to thee.

But now the cruel faithlessness
   That in thy breast I find,
Has shaken the devotedness
   I cherish'd in my mind:

So that I cannot love thee well,
   Though spotless thou shouldst shine;
Nor fond love's doting thoughts dispel,
   Though every fault were thine.

LXXVI.

TO HIMSELF.—THE LOVER'S PETITION.

If past good deeds,—if an unsullied fame,
    Unbroken faith, and fair integrity,
That ne'er to wrong mankind abused heaven's name,
    Wake in the breast of man sweet memory;

Then for long years to thee rich joys are due,
    Catullus, from this love, ah! ill-repaid;
For all that man could either say or do,
    With kindliest heart, by thee was done and said;

Yet all was lost upon the thankless fair;—
    Why more with tortures, then, be rack'd and riven?
Come, steel thy heart, withdraw thee from the snare,
    And cease to be a wretch in spite of heaven.

'Tis hard to quench at once a long-nursed love;
    'Tis hard—but do it howsoe'er you may;
It is your only chance—your courage prove—
    Easy or difficult—you must obey.

Ye gods! if pity in your bosoms dwell,
    Or if to man ye e'er deliverance bear
When death's dark whelming billows round him swell,
    Oh! look on me, and hear a wretch's prayer;

And, if a stainless life the boon may claim,
　　Oh! pluck from me this canker-worm and pest,
Which, like a torpor creeping through my frame,
　　Has banish'd every pleasure from my breast.

I ask not that she should return my love,
　　Or e'en be chaste—for that can never be:
Grant me but health, this fell disease remove,
　　Ye gods! with this repay my piety.

———◆———

LXXVII.

TO RUFUS.

Rufus! how fruitless and how vain
　　　My trust in thee:
Fruitless? nay, fraught with heavy gain
　　　Of woe to me.

Like reptile vile into my breast
　　　Didst thou thus stray,
And, wearing out my vitals, wrest
　　　My all away!

Alas! my every joy thou 'st ta'en,
　　　Life's upas-tree!
Alas, alas! my friendship's bane!
　　　Woe! woe is me!

Oh, now I grieve the spotless lip
    Of one so true
Was ever lured by thee to sip
    Thy mouth's foul dew.

Thou 'lt rue thy deed: all time in scorn
    Shall hold thy name,
And hoary fame to years unborn
    Shall speak thy shame.

LXXVIII.

ON GALLUS.

Gallus has two brothers: one
    Has a charming wife,
And the other has a son
    Full of mirth and life.

Gallus is a wag: and why?
    He, to crown their joy,
Gets the charming wife to lie
    With the charming boy.

Gallus is a fool: and, vext,
    He will scratch his head,
Should he find his nephew next
    With his wife a-bed.

LXXIX.

ON LESBIUS.

LESBIUS is fair: why not? in Lesbia's love,
Catullus! thee and all thy race above:
Yet me and all my kindred let him sell
If he but find three *men* to wish him well.

LXXX.

TO GELLIUS.

GELLIUS! why are thy lips, once rosy red,
    Hueless and paler than the winter snows,
Whether from home at early morn thou 'st sped,
    Or left thy couch from noontide's sweet repose?
I know not. Or is rumour's whisper true,
    That wanton joys your whole time occupy?
These pale the lips, how fresh soe'er their hue,
    And dim the lustre of the brightest eye.
[But now I grieve my pure girl's pure lips e'er
    Imbibed the slaver of a wretch like thee.
Thou 'lt rue it: ages on thy name shall bear,
    And hoary fame declare thine infamy.]

LXXXI.

TO A BEAUTY.

Fair maid! among
So vast a throng
　Couldst thou descry
No other swain,
Whom thou couldst deign
　With love to eye,

Than that low scamp,
From out the damp
　Pisauran vale?
The gilded sheen
Of bust, I ween,
　Was ne'er so pale.

He now enchains
Thy heart, and reigns
　Preferr'd to me.
Thy error, oh!
Thou dost not know,
　Alas for thee!

LXXXII.

TO QUINTIUS.

QUINTIUS! if thou wouldst have me owe to thee
Mine eyes, or aught, if aught's more dear to me,
Snatch not from me my soul's far dearer prize,
If aught there be still dearer than mine eyes.

LXXXIII.

ON THE HUSBAND OF LESBIA.

LESBIA says many ill things of me when her husband
    is present;
This to the poor silly fool is a thing most uncommonly
    pleasant;
Mule! you don't see it all: if silent she were and for-
    getful,
Free from love she might be; but now that she storms
    and is fretful,
She not remembers me only, but, what is a thing far
    severer,
Angry she is, so she burns, and still speaks of me:
    What can be clearer?

LXXXIV.

ON ARRIUS.

ARRIUS *commodious* aye *chommodious* call'd,
And for *insidious* out *hinsidious* bawl'd,
And then he thought his accent wondrous good
When he had mouth'd them rough as e'er he could.
His mother, and his uncle Liber, too,
And their good parents thus, methinks, would do.
He went to Syria,—all our ears had then
A sweet repose,—smooth flow'd the words again,
Vanish'd the fears that put us nigh distraught,
When, suddenly, the direful news was brought,
That Arrius, when in Syria, said that he
Just came from crossing the *Hionian* Sea.

LXXXV.

ON HIS LOVE.

I HATE and love. "Why do I so?"
    Perhaps you ask. I can't explain:
The bitter fact I only know,
    And torture racks my brain.

LXXXV.

(ANOTHER VERSION.)

I HATE and love. Why so? I cannot tell:
I feel it; and endure the pains of hell.

LXXXVI.

QUINTIA AND LESBIA COMPARED.

QUINTIA I know the many rate
   A gem of loveliness;
To me she's fair, and tall, and straight,
   These singly I confess;

But I that wondrous whole deny,
   Its line I fail to trace;
For where in that great figure lie
   The piquancy and grace?

Lesbia is lovely; she so rare—
   So beautiful withal,
Robb'd all her sex of all things fair,
   To wear the coronal.

LXXXVII. TRANSLATED IN LXXV.—

LXXXVIII.

ON GELLIUS.

Gellius! know'st thou the awful wickedness
Of him who yields to incest's mad caress?
'Tis such that all the waters of the main
Can ne'er obliterate the monstrous stain.
No guilt, how dark soe'er it be, can stretch
Beyond the baseness of the abandon'd wretch.

LXXXIX.

ON GELLIUS.

Gellius is thin: and what wonder? when he
    Has so blithe and so buxom a mother,
And a sister as lovely as maiden can be,
    Sooth! 'twould beat you to find such another.

And then he's an uncle so good and so green,
    And of she-cousins such a bright bevy,
'Twould rather be strange if he were not so lean,
    Their demands on him *must* be so heavy.

For although he *should never* a woman embrace
Save the very same ones he *should never*,
You'll find good enough reason, I trow, why his face
Should be lean and still leaner than ever.

XC.

ON GELLIUS.

LET Gellius' and his mother's lust be crown'd
With one who shall the Persians' creed expound,
For Magian must from son and mother rise,
If truth in Persia's vile religion lies;
To venerate with accents meet heaven's name,
And melt the fat omentum in the flame.

XCI.

ON GELLIUS.

No, Gellius! never did I hope thou'dst prove
Faithful in this my wretched, frenzied love,
Because I knew thee well, nor thought thy mind
Could be restrain'd from vice of any kind,
But that my ardent love—'twas this alone—
Was nursed for no relation of thine own;

And though I knew thee well, I never dream'd
That thou wouldst this a fit pretext have deem'd.
Thou thought'st so : such with thee is vice's gust,
That nothing 'scapes thy foul, insatiate lust.

XCII.

ON LESBIA.

Lesbia rails against me ever,
And of me is silent never,
May I die if Lesbia loves me not sincerely.
Why ? Don't I do the same,
And aye malign her name ?
But may I die if I don't love her dearly.

XCIII.

ON CAESAR.

To please you, Caesar, I don't care one plack,
Nor care I whether you are white or black.

XCIV.

ON MAMURRA.

Mamurra sins: Mamurra is a sot:
The proverb's true: Herbs grow to fill the pot.

XCV.

ON "SMYRNA," A POEM BY CINNA.

Nine harvests since was Cinna's work begun,
Nine winters see at last his "Smyrna" done;
Whereas Hortensius, in a single year,
Throws off five hundred thousand verses clear.
"Smyrna" will charm where Satrachus doth roll,
And times unborn will read the labour'd scroll;
Volusius' Annals shall in Padua die,
Or in its shops for mack'rel wrappers lie:
My friend's small labours to my heart are dear,
Turgid Antimachus the mob may cheer.

XCVI.

TO CALVUS, ON THE DEATH OF QUINTILIA.

CALVUS! if from our grief aught can accrue
    The silent dead to solace or to cheer,
When fond regret broods o'er old loves anew,
    And o'er lost friendships sheds the bitter tear;

Oh! then her grief at death's untimely blow
    To thy Quintilia far, far less must prove
Than the pure joy her soul must feel, to know
    Thy true, unchanging, ever-during love.

XCVII.

ON AEMILIUS.

By heaven! without a word of jesting,
I really could not help protesting,
Were I desired to kiss that flunkey:
Egad! I'd rather kiss a monkey!
His mouth, you see, is not the cleanest,
His *tout-ensemble* is the meanest;

But, if I needs *must* kiss the noddy,
I'd choose some portion of his body
Where grinders did not stare before me,
Like lethal weapons meant to gore me.
Teeth! why their length is full six inches;
Gums! like a pair of rotten benches;
Besides, when he is grinning, marry!
The orifice is like a quarry.
Yet he to this or that cit's daughter
Pays court, and proudly boasts he's caught her,
Whereas the dolt, exiled from lasses,
Should drive the mill with kindred asses;
The girl who for her mate would choose him
Might take a hangman to her bosom.

XCVIII.

TO VETTIUS.

All that is said to fools and prattlers dire,
  O foul-mouth'd Vettius! may be said to you,
For with that tongue of yours, should need require,
  You'd lick the cow-boy's filth-bedabbled shoe.
If ruin fell on all you wish to send,
Just wag your tongue: you're sure to gain your end[1]

XCIX.

THE KISS.—TO A BEAUTY.

FAIR honey'd maid! the while you play'd
  I stole a little kiss,
And sweet ambrosia could not match
  The sweetness of my bliss.

For that fond raid I dearly paid,
  For hourly more and more,
What pains the cross-nail'd wretch endures,
  Such agonies I bore.

I pleaded love—in vain I strove;
  No grief, no tears of mine
Could drive away one jot of that
  Hard-heartedness of thine.

Whene'er 'twas done, too cruel one!
  Thy little lips were rinsed,
And by each finger of thy hand
  With every effort cleansed,

Till not a trace on thy sweet face
  From lip of mine remain'd,
As if some vicious profligate
  Its purity had stain'd.

Nay more: thy spite 'tis thy delight
    In every way to vent,
And never hast thou ceased my heart
    To torture and torment.

That this wee kiss might smack of bliss
    Ambrosian never more,
But be more bitter to my soul
    Than bitter hellebore.

Since such the pains thy heart ordains
    To my sad love, I swear,
I'll never steal a kiss again,
    Nor tamper with the fair.

C.

ON COELIUS AND QUINTIUS.

Young Coelius and Quintius, the beauty
    And flower of the Veronese youth,
To two sisters are paying love's duty—
    A bond right fraternal, in sooth.

Whose suit shall my best wish attend?
    Thine, Coelius! for thou wast well tried
At the time I most needed a friend:
    Then, Coelius, be blest in thy bride.

CI.

THE POET AT HIS BROTHER'S GRAVE.

BROTHER! o'er many lands and oceans borne,
I reach thy grave, death's last sad rite to pay;
To call thy silent dust in vain, and mourn,
Since ruthless fate has hurried thee away:
Woe's me! yet now upon thy tomb I lay,
All soak'd with tears for thee, thee loved so well,
What gifts our fathers gave the honour'd clay
Of valued friends; take them, my grief they tell:
And now, for ever hail! for ever fare-thee-well!

CI.

(From the text of Schwabe.)

BORNE over many a land and many a sea,
    Brother! I reach thy gloom-wrapt grave to pay
The last sad office thou may'st claim from me,
    And all in vain address thy silent clay:

For thou art gone—fell fate that from me tore
    Thee, thee, my brother! ah, too cruel thought!
I'll call thee, but I'll never hear thee more
    Recount the deeds thy valiant arm hath wrought.

And I shall never see thy face again,
   Dearer than life; yet in my heart alway
Assuredly shall fond affection reign,
   And aye with grief's wan hues I'll tinge my lay:

Yea, even as the Daulian bird her song
   Outpours in accents sweetly-dolorous,
When o'er the branch-gloom'd river, all night long,
   She wails the fate of perish'd Itylus.

Yet now what gifts our sires in ancient years
   Paid those with whom in life they loved to dwell,
Accept:—all streaming with thy brother's tears;
   And, brother! hail for aye! for aye farewell!

CII.

TO CORNELIUS.

IF e'er true friend a secret darẹd disclose
   To silent friend of known fidelity,
Thou'lt find me of the brotherhood of those:
   Harpocrates could not more silent be.

CIII.

TO SILO.

Silo! return my hundred pounds, I pray,
Then be as fierce and savage as you may:
Or cease, if money's all in all to you,
To be a pimp, and fierce and savage too.

CIV.

ON LESBIA.

What! *I* my love, my very life malign,
   Who's dearer far to me than both mine eyes?
No: that could never be with love like mine,
   But you with Tappo frame a world of lies.

CV.

ON MAMURRA.

Mamurra fain would soar to Pimpla's crown,
The Muses with their pitchforks chuck him down.

CVI.

ON AN AUCTIONEER AND A PRETTY GIRL.

WHOEVER sees a salesman with a belle
Must surely think he's brought her out to sell.

CVII.

TO LESBIA.—THE RECONCILIATION.

IF e'er that wish which mortal holds most dear
   Hath by his eager, longing heart been gain'd,
When not a gleam of hope remain'd to cheer;
   The boon how sweet! the pleasure how unfeign'd!

Such is the sweet, unfeign'd delight I feel—
   Which wealth of glittering gold could ne'er impart—
To know my Lesbia, reconciled and leal,
   Will now be press'd to my enraptured heart.

To my fond arms, and of thine own accord,
   Thou comest after hope's last ray had fled;
A whiter mark shall the pure bliss record,
   This happy day upon my life hath shed.

Who is there boasts a happier fate than mine ?
  Or rather, where is he would not declare
The lot that binds my destiny with thine,
  Compared with that of others, passing fair?

CVIII.

ON COMINIUS.

If thy impure gray hairs to death should be,
Cominius, doom'd by popular decree,
I trow that first thy tongue, that loathes the good,
Cut out, should glut the vulture's ravenous brood ;
Thine eyes should gorge the raven's sable maw ;
Dogs should thy bowels, wolves the remnants gnaw.

CIX.

TO LESBIA.

My life ! thou swear'st no trials e'er shall change
Our honey'd love, nor years our hearts estrange.
Truth to her vows, Almighty Heaven ! impart ;
Oh, be her words sincere, and from the heart ;
That all our lives our souls may faithful prove
In this eternal bond of holy love.

CX.

TO AUFILENA.

O Aufilène, we've ever seen
    True, honest sweethearts praised,
Our gifts they take, nor lightly break
    The darling hopes they've raised.

Oh, 'twas unfair in thee to swear
    Thou 'dst give a kiss to me;
My gift to take, and then to break
    Thy word: 'twas base in thee.

An honest maid had not delay'd
    The payment sweet to bring;
A modest queen might not have been
    So quick in promising.

To prowl for prey, and skulk away,
    Smacks of the wanton's art,
Who's ever fain, for paltry gain,
    To play the meanest part.

CXI.

TO AUFILENA.

O AUFILENA! 'tis a wife's best praise,
   Pleased with one lord to live and love no other;
But if you needs must stray from virtue's ways,
   Oh, never, never be your cousins' mother.

CXII.

TO NASO.

NASO, thou 'rt great, as greatness goes with thee:
Naso, thou 'rt great in lust and infamy.

CXIII.

TO CINNA.

CINNA, when Pompey first was consul, none
Save two as Mucia's paramours were known;
In Pompey's second consulship each one
Could count his pupils to a thousand grown;
This crop full well repays the sower's toil:
The seed will spring and thrive in any soil.

CXIV.

ON MAMURRA.

MAMURRA! justly, from your lands,
    You're deem'd a wealthy lord;
For all that lordly wealth commands
    Your Formian fields afford.

Fishes, beasts, birds of every breed,
    Plough'd fields and meadow grounds;
'Tis all in vain: your debts exceed
    Your fortune's utmost bounds.

I grant your income may be great:
    Want holds you aye in thrall;
The owner of a fine estate!
    A beggar with it all!

CXV.

ON MAMURRA.

FORMIAN of thirty acres is possest
In meadow-land; ploughed, forty; seas the rest:
Why is he not in wealth o'er Croesus crown'd?
Such countless stores he reckons at a bound:

Meads, fields, vast woods, lawns, marshy grounds beside,
Far as the frozen North, as Ocean wide.
All these are great: yet yield to him they must;
A man! oh, no: a universe of lust!

CXVI.

TO GELLIUS.

OFT have I wish'd the lays of Battus' son
To send for thee with studious mind to con,
That I might calm thy bitter spleen, and stay
The darts thou hurlest at my head alway.
O Gellius! now I see my toil was vain,
And that my prayers had fail'd thine ear to gain:
'Neath my strong mail I'll shun thy every dart,
But mine shall pierce and lacerate thy heart.

EXCURSUS

AND

ILLUSTRATIVE NOTES.

EXCURSUS

AND

ILLUSTRATIVE NOTES.

POEM I.

CATULLUS modestly dedicates his little work (lepidum novum libellum) to his friend and fellow-countryman Cornelius Nepos, author of "Lives of Illustrious Commanders," and a "Universal History," in three books. The latter work, which was probably given to the world about B.C. 50, has perished.

CARM. I. v. 9.*
———O patrona Virgo,
    Virgo=Minerva.
Cf. Hor. Epist. ad Pisones, 385.
    Tu nihil invita dices faciesve Minerva.

* In giving the parallel notes reference is made throughout to the lines of the original.

Poems II. and III.

These two exquisite little poems have been the admiration of scholars and men of taste both in ancient and modern times. The playful tenderness, delicacy, and inimitable grace which they evince throughout impart to them a special charm.

The following short poem by Martial, (Epigr. i. 110,) though by no means equal to either of the famous songs of Catullus, is nevertheless one of the prettiest of the many "Nugae canorae" in imitation of the "Sparrow:"—

> Issa than Catullus' sparrow
>   Far more frolic is,
> Issa's purer, purer far, oh!
>   Than the dove's pure kiss;
> Blander far than maiden fair,
> Than the gems of Ind more rare,
> Issa! Issa! darling bright,
> Issa, Publius' delight.
>
> If you heard pet Issa whimper
>   You would think she spake,
> Grief and joy her whine and simper
>   Tell beyond mistake.
> On his neck her nap she takes,
> Not a breath the silence breaks,
> All so still and cosily
> Does his charming Issa lie.
>
> With entreating paw she taps you,
>   And the darling pup
> Prays, "put me to bed," "perhaps you
>   Now will raise me up."
> Innocence's paragon!
> Love her heart hath never known,
> Nor have we discover'd yet
> Lover worthy of our pet.

Publius, 'lest death should strike her,
Had her painted; lo!
You'll see Issa limn'd so like her
That you could not know.
Place her by the picture there,
I aver you will declare
You've two living Issas seen,
Or that both have painted been.

CARM. II. v. 13.
Quod zonam soluit diu ligatum.

Thus imitated in the "Priapeia," (Anthologia Latina, Carm. 1704. Edit. Meyer) :—

Te vocant prece virgines pudicae,
Zonulam ut solüas diu ligatam.

CARM. III. v. 5.
Quem plus illa oculis suis amabat.

Cf. Theoc. Idyll. xi. 53 :—
Καὶ τὸν ἕν' ὀφθαλμόν, τῷ μοι γλυκερώτερον οὐδέν.

V. 13-15.
At ——— abstulistis.

Cf. Ov. Amor. ii. 6, 37-40.

Occidit ille loquax, humanae vocis imago
Psittacus, extremo munus ab orbe datum.
Optima prima fere manibus rapiuntur avaris,
Implentur numeris deteriora suis.

Dead! my pretty chatterer,
That mimick'd human sounds,
Parrot! sent to me ye were
From earth's remotest bounds;
Ever first our fairest joy
By ruthless hand is ta'en;
Countless things of base alloy
Are fated to remain.

And Bion, Idyll. i. 55.
τόδε πᾶν καλὸν ἐς σὲ καταρρεῖ.

V. 17, 18.   Tua ——— ocelli.

Cf. Mart. Epigr. vii. 14:—

 Oh! a dire misfortune, Aulus,
  Comes my charmer's joys to blight;
 She has lost her darling playmate,
  She has lost her heart's delight.

 Such the tender bard Catullus'
  Lovely Lesbia did not mourn,
 In the frolic little sparrow
  From her fond caresses torn;

 Or my Stella, in the dove that
  Cost Ianthis many a tear,
 And which now throughout Elysium
  Flits, a shadow dark and drear.

 Ne'er such trifles, ne'er such playthings
  Won my lovely charmer's heart;
 Never did her tender bosom
  From such trivial losses smart.

 She has lost a youth of twenty
  Summers, all his peers above,
 Who had never learn'd to wander
  In the fairy realms of love.

Mart. Epigr. xiv. 77. "Cavea eborea."

 Si tibi talis erit, qualem dilecta Catullo
  Lesbia plorabat, hic habitare potest.
 If yours a sparrow such as Lesbia, dear
  To young Catullus, mourn'd, confine it here.

Juvenal alludes to this poem, Sat. vi. 7, 8:—

 ——— haud similis tibi, Cynthia, nec tibi, cujus
  Turbavit nitidos extinctus passer ocellos.

POEM IV.

CATULLUS sings the praises of the yacht in which he sailed home from Amastris to Sirmio. He had just completed his tour to the famous cities of Asia, after leaving Bithynia, whither he had gone in the company of the Praetor Caius Memmius Gemellus. In the present poem he mentions the principal places in the course of his voyage in inverted order (verses 6-10), and, after eulogising the sea-worthiness of his yacht, concludes by dedicating her to the twin-gods Castor and Pollux, determined that he shall not again expose her to the dangers of the deep, but allow her to enjoy an honoured age on the waters of Benacus (Lago di Garda).

CARM. IV. v. 9-11.
   Ponticum ——— silva.
Cf. Hor. Od. i. 14, 11-13.
   Quamvis Pontica pinus,
   Silvae filia nobilis,
  Jactes et genus et nomen inutile.

V. 11, 12.
  ————nam Cytorio in jugo
  Loquente saepe sibilum edidit coma.

Cf. Theoc. Idyll. i. 1 :—
  Ἀδύ τι τὸ ψιθύρισμα καὶ ἁ πίτυς.
And Virg. Ecl. v. 28.
  ——— silvaeque loquuntur.

V. 13. Amastri Pontica et Cytore buxifer.
Amastris, so called from the niece of Darius, the last king of Persia, and wife of Dionysius, tyrant of Heraclea, anciently Sesamos, now *Amasserah*, was situated on the shores of the Pontus Euxinus (*Black Sea*), a few miles to the east of the Par-

thenius. A little to the east of it was Cytorus (*Kidros*), at the foot of Mount Cytorus (*Afar Dag*), famous for boxwood (buxifer.)

Virg. Geor. ii. 437.
> Et juvat undantem buxo spectare Cytorum.

Poem V.

CATULLUS calls on Lesbia to come and enjoy with him the delights of love. From the closing lines of the poem he seems to have been a believer in the popular superstition of all ages and countries—the blasting power of envy.

CARM. V. v. 1.
> Vivamus, mea Lesbia, atque amemus.

Cf. Tibull. i. 1, 69-72.
> Interea, dum fata sinunt, jungamus amores :
> Jam veniet tenebris Mors adoperta caput,
> Jam subrepet iners aetas, neque amare decebit,
> Dicere nec cano blanditias capiti.

> Love's joys be ours while still the fates allow,
> Soon death will come with darkly-mantled head,
> Dull age creeps on; and love-kiss or love-vow
> Beseems no forehead, where its snows are shed.

And Prop. iii. 7, 23-26 (ii. 15, 23-26.)
> Dum nos fata sinunt, oculos satiemus amore,
> Nox tibi longa venit nec reditura dies.
> Atque utinam haerentes sic nos vincire catena
> Velles, ut nunquam solveret ulla dies!

> While fate allows, let love our fond eyes sate,
> A long night comes, and no returning day;

> Oh, would that love around us both might plait
> A clasping chain that will endure for aye !

V. 4–6.   Soles —— dormienda.

Cf. Hor. iv. 7, 13–16.

> Damna tamen celeres reparant caelestia lunae ;
>   Nos, ubi decidimus,
> Quo pius Aeneas, quo dives Tullus et Ancus,
>   Pulvis et umbra sumus.

> The fleet moons wane again to gem the sky ;
>   But we, when we are laid
> Where good Aeneas, Tullus, Ancus lie,
>   Are only dust and shade.

Mosch. Idyll. iii. 109-111.

> Ἄμμες δ' οἱ μεγάλοι καὶ καρτεροί, οἱ σοφοὶ ἄνδρες
> Ὁππότε πρᾶτα θάνωμες, ἀνάκοοι ἐν χθονὶ κοίλᾳ
> Εὔδομες εὖ μάλα μακρὸν ἀτέρμονα νήγρετον ὕπνον.

> But we, the great, the brave, the wise of men,
> When we have pass'd away from mortal ken,
> Must slumber in earth's hollow chamber housed,
> One long eternal night, unheard-of, unaroused.

And Burns—
> Cheerless night that knows no morrow.

V. 7.   Da mihi basia mille, &c.

Cf. Chaucer, " Wyf of Bathes Tale"—

> And whan the knyght saugh verrayly al this
> That sche so fair was and so yong therto,
> For joye he hent hir in his armes two,
> His herte bathid in a bath of blisse,
> A thousand tyme on rowe he gan hir kisse.

Mart. xi. 6, 14-16.

> Da mihi basia sed Catulliana :
> Quae si tot fuerint, quot ille dixit,
> Donabo tibi passerem Catulli.

> Now give me kisses such as Lesbia lipp'd,
> And young Catullus erst divinely sipp'd,

And, if his countless number should be mine,
I vow Catullus' sparrow shall be thine.

Id. xii. 59, 1-3.

Tantum dat tibi Roma basiorum
Post annos modo quindecim reverso,
Quantum Lesbia non dedit Catullo.

Fifteen years away—now Rome
  My lips does with her kisses cumber;
Lesbia, aye in love at home,
  Ne'er gave Catullus half the number.

V. 13.   Cum tantum sciat esse basiorum.

Imitated in the Priapeia, 52, 12. (Anth. Lat., Meyer, 1667.)
Cum tantum hic sciet esse mentularum.

POEM VI.

CATULLUS rallies his friend Flavius on the object of his affections, and in a humorous effusion entreats him to tell him her name, that he may embalm them both in a lively lay.

Of Flavius nothing whatever is known.

CARM. VI. v. 15, 16.   Quare——nobis.

Cf. Hor. Od. i. 27, 17.

Quidquid habes, age,
Depone tutis auribus.

ILLUSTRATIVE NOTES. 185

POEM VII.

THIS poem, red-hot from the furnace of passion, is the poet's answer to a question of Lesbia's. It concludes with an allusion to the occult influence of envy similar to that in Carm. V.

Martial has imitated this poem in some very pretty lines, (Epigr. vi. 34) :—

> O Diadumene! come, kiss, and kiss me more and more;
> How oft? As well say count the waves that ocean fill,
> The myriad shells that scatter'd lie on the Aegean shore,
> And bees that wander o'er Hymettus' flowery hill,
> Or in the crowded theatre the cheers or hands that wave
> When all the people see a-sudden Caesar come;
> I will not have what sweet Catullus ask'd and Lesbia gave:
> Few are the joys he craves who number can the sum.

CARM. VII. v. 4.

Laserpiciferis ―――― Cyrenis.

Cyrene (*Ghrennah*), the chief city of Cyrenaica, founded by Battus, (B.C. 631.)

V. 5. Oraculum Jovis inter aestuosi.

The famous oracle of Jupiter (Ammon) here referred to was situated in the oasis of Ammonium (*Siwah*), in the Libyan desert.

Cf. with verses 3-8 of this poem, Catull. xlviii., and Ovid. Epist. ex Ponto, ii. 7, 23-30.

> Crede mihi, si sum veri tibi cognitus oris,
>   Ne numeros nostris casibus esse putes,
> Cinyphiae segetis citius numerabis aristas,
>   Altaque quam multis floreat Hybla thymis :
> Et quot aves motis nitantur in aëre pennis,
>   Quotque natent pisces aequore, certus eris,

> Quam tibi nostrorum statuatur summa laborum,
> Quos ego sum terra, quos ego passus aqua.

If thou in me a truthful man hast known,
Think not my woes can be by numbers shown,
Thou 'lt sooner sum Cinyphia's ears of corn,
The flowers of thyme that Hybla's hills adorn,
The feather'd tribes that boundless ether skim,
The myriad fishes that in ocean swim,—
Than all my woes by thee shall number'd be,
The woes I 've borne by land—the woes I 've borne by sea.

Poem VIII.

CATULLUS awakens from his dream of bliss. Lesbia is false. She has been fooling him. He cannot endure it. He consoles himself with the thought that she once loved him; that he once loved her; but it is all over now—

> Fulsere quondam candidi tibi soles.

He bids her farewell for ever, and vows henceforward to remain insensible to the witchery of her charms. He pictures the wretchedness of her future life, the loneliness of her lot; the hues of beauty fading from her cheek; love grown cold, and all its joys for ever blighted; and declares once more his firm and unshaken resolve. Yet, all her faithlessness notwithstanding, he cannot think of Lesbia as the mistress of another. How different the feelings of Catullus in this poem from those of his great successor in the realm of lyric poetry, when he bids farewell to the beautiful Neaera. (Epod. xv.) :—

> 'Twas night; and in the starry sky
> The moon was shining clear,

When thou to mock the gods on high
    Didst whisper in mine ear,
The while my neck encircling with those soft white arms of thine,
More close than ivy sprays around the stately ilex twine.

" So long as flocks the wolf shall flee,
    And as Orion's star,
Wild-harassing the wintry sea,
    Affrights the mariner,
Yea, while the gentle breeze fans young Apollo's streaming hair,
So long our love shall constant be, so long mine own! I swear."

Alas! thou 'lt mourn my slighted truth,
    For know, while honour's mine,
I ne'er will suffer rival youth
    To press his heart to thine.
Another shall be mine; farewell! my sure resolve once ta'en,
Thy hated beauty ne'er will shake my fixedness again.

Go, happier swain, thy pathway hold,
    Exulting o'er my woe,
Though thine be flocks and lands untold—
    For thee Pactolus flow:
Though learnèd as the Samian thou—to thee fair Nireus vile,
With tears thou'lt curse the fickle jade, while I in turn shall smile.

CARM. VIII.

Compare with this and the later poems to Lesbia. Ovid. Amor. iii. 11.

Much, long I bore: my patience is outworn;
    Leave my worn heart, base love, thy reign is o'er;
I'm free, my fetters I've asunder torn,
    I blush I've borne what I unblushing bore.

I've conquer'd, and I trample conquer'd love;
    Too long I wore a too complacent brow.
Endure; be steel; thy woe thy weal will prove,
    Oft bitter draughts have soothed the wretch ere now.

So oft repulsed thy portal, did I place
    My freeborn body on the cold damp stone?

Did I, while one received thy fond embrace,
   Guard like a slave thy closèd door alone?

I've seen thy lover, weak in every limb,
   Like jaded veteran from thy threshold go;
This pain was light; but to be seen of him!
   May such disgrace, ye gods! befall my foe.

When, patiently, have I not to thee clung?
   Thou hadst a guardian, lover, friend, in me,
Thou wast beloved because thy charms I'd sung,
   My love made many a lover dote on thee.

Why should I tell thy vain tongue's impious lies?
   Thy broken oaths attested by the gods?
Or at the board thy bland, deceitful guise,
   Thy preconcerted signs and silent nods?

They said, "She's sick," to thee I frantic sped,
   There was no sickness when my rival came;
From these and other wrongs my heart hath bled,
   Go find another who will bear the same.

My vessel now, with votive garlands crown'd,
   Hears, safely moor'd, the dashing billows' roar;
Hence with thy fondling words of spell-like sound,
   I am no more the fool I was before.

Hatred and love my troubled bosom fill,
   But love, methinks, with fiercer fury burns;
I'll willing hate, else love against my will;
   The steer disdains yet bears the yoke he spurns.

I flee thy vileness, and thy charms adore,
   Detest thy crimes, before thy beauty kneel;
With or without thee life is life no more,
   I seem to know not what I think or feel.

Would thou hadst virtue more or charms less bright,
   Such beauty ill-beseems a course so base,

Hatred thy deeds, but love thy charms excite,
  Ah, me! thy face thy falseness far outweighs.

Oh, spare me by the rights of love, and by
  The gods invoked in those false vows of thine,
And by thy face—a mighty deity—
  And by thy radiant eyes that ravish'd mine.

Be what thou wilt, mine thou shalt ever be,
  Choose 'tween a love against or with my will,
My sails are spread, winds, waft us o'er life's sea,
  For, though I would not, I must love thee still.

V. 3.   Fulsere quondam candidi tibi soles.

Cf. Burns—
  Farewell hours that late did measure
  Sunshine days of joy and pleasure.

V. 14, &c.
  At tu dolebis, cum rogaberis nulla.
  Scelesta! vae te! Quae tibi manet vita?

Cf. Tibull. i. 8, 39-46.
  Non lapis hanc gemmaeque juvant, quae frigore sola
    Dormiat et nulli sit cupienda viro.
  Heu sero revocatur amor seroque juventa,
    Cum vetus infecit cana senecta caput.
  Tum studium formae est: coma tum mutatur, ut annos
    Dissimulet viridi cortice tincta nucis:
  Tollere tum cura est albos a stirpe capillos
    Et faciem dempta pelle referre novam.

  Rich stones and gems can ne'er her heart engage,
    Who in the cold, all undesired, sleeps lone;
  Too late are love and youth recall'd, when age
    The snows of winter o'er the head hath strown.
  Then comes the rage for beauty, then the care
    With green-nut-husk the changèd locks to stain,

> To wipe out years, to pluck each silver hair,
> To make the wither'd cheek bloom fresh again.

Id. i. 9, 77 to the end—
> Blanditiasne meas aliis tu vendere es ausus,
> Tune aliis demens oscula ferre mea?
> Tunc flebis cum me vinctum puer alter habebit
> Et geret in regno regna superba tuo.
>
> At tua tum me poena juvet, Venerique merenti
> Fixa notet casus aurea palma meos.
> "Hanc tibi fallaci resolutus amore Tibullus
> Dedicat et grata sis, dea, mente rogat."

> To other lovers hast thou dared impart
> The joys, the kisses due to me alone,
> Thou'lt weep when one more leal enchains my heart,
> And proudly sways my breast, once all thine own.
>
> Thy pain will glad my soul—a golden shield
> To Venus, my protectress, shall proclaim:
> "From glad Tibullus, saved from love's fell field,
> Who prays thy favour and reveres thy name."

V. 18.
> Quem basiabis? quoi labella mordebis?

Cf. Hor. Od. i. 13, 11–15.
> . . . . sive puer furens
> Impressit memorem dente labris notam.
> Non, si me satis audias,
> Speres perpetuum, dulcia barbare
> Laedentem oscula.

And Tibull. i. 6, 13, 14.
> Tunc succos herbasque dedi, quis livor abiret,
> Quem facit impresso mutua dente Venus.
>
> I gave her herbs and juices, to remove
> The leaden traces of the tooth of love.

Poem IX.

This exquisite little poem, every line of which is redolent of rare and disinterested friendship, is addressed to a young man, of whom little is known except the name. He had gone to Spain in the suite of Piso, but, owing to the greediness and meanness of his superior, the calling he had chosen proved anything but a lucrative one.

Carm. IX. v. 9.
    Jucundum os, oculosque suaviabor.

Cf. Homer. Odyss. xvi. 15.
    Κύσσε δέ μιν κεφαλήν τε καὶ ἄμφω φάεα καλά.
Compare with this poem, *passim*, Hor. Od. i. 36.

———◆———

Poem X.

Catullus has just returned from Bithynia, whither he had gone in the suite of Caius Memmius Gemellus, to whose knavery he in great measure attributes his own ill-fortune and that of his companions. Memmius, to whom Lucretius dedicated his noble poem " De Rerum Natura," was as distinguished for culture and scholarly attainments as for grasping meanness, profligacy, and extravagance.

Whether the Varus of this poem is Alphenus Varus, (Cremonensis), the lawyer, or Quintilius Varus, (Cremonensis), the friend of Horace and Virgil, it is impossible to say. Most of the commentators think the former is the person referred to.

CARM. X. v. 20.
      Non possem octo homines parare rectos.
Cf. Mart. ix. 3-11.
      Octo Syris suffulta datur lectica puellae.

———◆———

POEM XI.

CATULLUS, in a somewhat lengthy but magnificent exordium, pays a high tribute to the tried friendship of Furius and Aurelius.

Firm in his resolve to abandon Lesbia for ever, he intrusts the parting message to these friends. In the injunction—
      Pauca nuntiate *meae* puellae
      Non bona dicta,

we can distinguish traces of a lingering fondness. Catullus cannot bear the thought that she should cherish affection for another, and prays that, although she may be surrounded by hundreds of admirers, her heart may be, for ever, dead to love.

The beautiful image of the share-crushed flower, in the last stanza, has been repeatedly imitated.

CARM. XI. v. 1, *seqq.*
      Furi et Aureli comites Catulli.
Cf. Hor. Od. ii. 6, 1-4.
      Septimi, Gades aditure mecum, et
      Cantabrum indoctum juga ferre nostra, et
      Barbaras Syrtes, ubi Maura semper
            Aestuat unda.

V. 3.   Litus ut longe, &c.
      ut=ubi.

V. 21. . . . . velut prati
Ultimi flos, praetereunte postquam
Tactus aratro est.
Cf. Virg. Æn. ix. 435—
Purpureus veluti cum flos, succisus aratro,
Languescit moriens.

As when the purple flower, cut by the share,
Droops dying.

And Burns, "To a Mountain Daisy," *passim*.

———◆———

POEM XII.

MARRUCINUS ASINIUS, to whom this by no means complimentary poem is addressed, was the son of Cneius Asinius, and brother of the celebrated Caius Asinius Pollio. Whether Marrucinus is a *name* or an *epithet* it is difficult to say; but there is little doubt that Asinius was indebted for it to the circumstance that the *gens Asinia* originally belonged to *Teate*, the chief town of the *Marrucini*, a Marsic people inhabiting the district lying between the Vestini and Peligni.

While the poet deprecates the absurd behaviour of Marrucinus, he speaks in high terms of the honourable character and cheerful dispositions of Pollio. The latter afterwards played a distinguished part in the reign of Augustus, whose favour and friendship he gained. He was alike famous as soldier, orator, historian, and dramatic poet. Virgil and Horace enjoyed his patronage and intimacy. The former alludes with pride to Pollio's appreciation of the productions of his muse, and has inscribed to him his fourth Eclogue; while the latter, in the first ode of his Second Book, has paid a high tribute to his varied abilities. He died at his Tusculan villa A.D. 4, in the eightieth year of his age.

CARM. XII. verses 12, 13, 16, 17.
Quod me non movet aestimatione,
Verum est *mnemosynon* mei sodalis.
. . . . . Haec amem necesse est
Ut Veranniolum meum et Fabullum.

Cf. Ovid. Heroïd. xvii. 71, 72—
. . . . sic acceptissima semper
Munera sunt, auctor quae pretiosa facit.
So ever the receiver most doth prize
The gift whose value in the giver lies.

V. 14.   Nam sudaria Saetaba, &c.,

Saetabis, *Jativa*, a town of the Contestani in Hispania Tarraconensis, and a Roman municipium, celebrated for its linen manufactures, lay on a hill south of the Sucro.

———◆———

POEM XIII.

CATULLUS promises his friend a glorious dinner, if he will furnish the materials. In return for these he will give him an unguent, and such an unguent!

Quod tu cum olfacies, Deos rogabo,
Totum ut te faciant, Fabulle, nasum.

Horace invites his friend Virgil—whoever that "juvenum nobilium cliens" might be—to a somewhat similar entertainment, engaging to provide the "cask" if Virgil brings the "box of unguents."

Martial, in an amusing epigram, tells us of an entertainment given by a worthy in his day, who, like the

ILLUSTRATIVE NOTES. 195

friend of our poet, rejoiced in the name of Fabullus, at which there was nothing but unguents. (Epigr. iii. 12.)

> Unguentum, fateor, bonum dedisti
> Convivis here : sed nihil scidisti.
> Res salsa est, bene olere et esurire.
> Qui non coenat et ungitur, Fabulle,
> Hic vere mihi mortuus videtur.

> The guests you had for yesterday invited
> Were with your unguents, I confess, delighted ;
> But you had neither joint nor cold collation,
> 'Tis rather funny, perfumes and starvation ;
> Who nothing eats, but sits a perfumed dummy,
> Appears to me to be a perfect mummy.

The use of perfumes among the Romans was all but universal, and during the Empire the taste for them amounted to a frenzy. The Romans were entirely unacquainted with distillation till the time of Nero ; consequently they preserved the odours of flowers and herbs in oil. The coarser kinds were kept in shells (*conchae*), or bottles of a globular form (*ampullae*); the finer sorts in small vases made from a kind of gypsum (*alabastron. s. onyx*). Owing to the narrowness of the neck of the latter, the contents could only be got drop by drop, and when the whole was wanted at once it was necessary to break the bottle. (Cf. N. T., St Mark xiv. 3, and St Matt. xxvi. 7.)

Martial recommends that wine and perfumes should be enjoyed by the possessor, never left to heirs. (Epigr. xiii. 126.)

> Unguentum heredi nunquam, nec vina relinquas.
> Ille habeat nummos : haec tibi tota dato.

> Leave not thine heir thy perfumes or thy wine ;
> Leave him thy money : but let these be thine.

And again, with reference to the juice of the grape, (Epigr. vi. 27, 5, 6.)

> Tu tamen annoso nimium ne parce Falerno :
> Et potius plenos aere relinque cados.

> Stint not the produce of the Falern vine :
> Leave your casks fill'd with money, not with wine.

CARM. XIII. v. 1.
> Coenabis bene, mi Fabulle, apud me.

Cf. Mart. Epigr. xi. 52, 1.
> Coenabis belle, Juli Cerealis, apud me.

V. 9.   Sed contra accipies *meros amores*.

Cf. Mart. xiv. 206—"Cestos."
> Collo necte, puer, *meros amores*,
> Ceston de Veneris sinu calentem.

> This Cestus warm from Venus' breast, O boy!
> Twine round thy neck, 'tis love without alloy.

V. 11, 12.   Nam——Cupidinesque.

Cf. Propert. iii. 27, 15-18. (ii. 29, 15-18.)
> Quae cum Sidoniae nocturna ligamina mitrae
> Solverit atque oculos moverat illa graves,
> Adflabunt tibi non Arabum de gramine odores,
> Sed quos ipse suis fecit Amor manibus.

> When her Sidonian nightcap she unties,
> And opens up her slumber-laden eyes,
> Thou 'lt breathe no scents from herbs of Araby,
> But those that Love's own hands express'd for thee.

Poem XIV.

CAIUS LICINIUS MACER CALVUS, to whom this poem is addressed, was an orator and poet of great celebrity.

Tacitus, Cicero, and Seneca bear testimony to his abilities as an orator, and Aulus Gellius to his merits as a poet. His first great oratorical performance was the impeachment of Vatinius. (*Vide* Excursus to Carm. liii.)

His poetical productions bore a strong resemblance to those of Catullus in elegance, simplicity, and licentiousness.

Poem XVI.

IN this poem, addressed to Aurelius and Furius, the tried friends by whom he sent his farewell message to Lesbia, Catullus defends himself against the imputation of unchastity made by them against him. With regard to his verses he claims that licence ever accorded to the priest of the Muses. Ovid has done the same, (Trist. ii. 353, 354) :—

> Crede mihi, distant mores a carmine nostro :
> Vita verecunda est, Musa jocosa mea.

> Trust me, a twofold line your bard pursues,
> Pure is his life, but gamesome is his muse.

And Martial, in a pointed epigram (i. 36) addressed to his friend Cornelius, has laid down the law of the matter with sufficient clearness :—

> Cornelius, you complain my lays are loose,
> And unadapted to scholastic use ;

Why, just as in the case of man and wife,
The prick of pleasantry's their very life.
What! would you have me sing a bridal lay,
And in funereal words the theme essay?
At Flora's festival who robes him o'er,
And looks for white-stoled virtue in a whore?
Of sportive songs this ever was the law,
Unless they're spiced they are not worth a straw.
With your morose reflections, then, begone,
Leave my light themes and sportive jests alone,
Nor mutilate my books, I beg of you:
Priapus gelt! Egad! 'twould never do.

In addition to the passages cited above, compare the following:—

Mart. Epigr. i. 5, 7, 8—

Innocuos censura potest permittere lusus:
Lasciva est nobis pagina, vita proba est.

My harmless jokes the censor may endure:
My page is wanton, but my life is pure.

Ovid. Trist. ii. 363-370.

Quid, nisi cum multo Venerem confundere vino,
  Praecepit lyrici Teïa Musa senis?
Lesbia quid docuit Sappho nisi amare puellas?
  Tuta tamen Sappho, tutus et ille fuit.

Nec tibi, Battiade, nocuit, quod saepe legenti
  Delicias versu fassus es ipse tuas.
Fabula jucundi nulla est sine amore Menandri,
  Et solet hic pueris virginibusque legi.

"Blend love and rosy wine," the old Teian long
  Taught in his lyrics as ne'er taught another;
" Oh, love the girls," ran Lesbian Sappho's song,
  And no man question'd either one or t'other.

> Callimachus, it never harm'd thy lay
>   To tell the raptures of a heart love-laden;
> Where is the gay Menander's loveless play?
>   And yet he's read by boy and blushing maiden.

And again, v. 427-436— .
> Sic sua lascivo cantata est saepe Catullo
>   Femina, cui falsum Lesbia nomen erat.
> Nec contentus ea, multos vulgavit amores,
>   In quibus ipse suum fassus adulterium est.
> Par fuit exigui similisque licentia Calvi,
>   Detexit variis qui sua furta modis.
> Quid referam Ticidae, quid Memmi carmen, apud quos
>   Rebus adest nomen nominibusque pudor
> Cinna quoque his comes est, Cinnaque procacior Anser,
>   Et leve Cornifici parque Catonis opus.

> The wanton bard Catullus sang of yore
>   His charmer's praise in many a sportive ditty,
> Where she the feignèd name of Lesbia bore;
>   And, not contented with his sweetheart pretty,

> His many loves he publish'd far and near,
>   Confess'd his relish for forbidden pleasures;
> And little Calvus, too, in this his peer,
>   Has told us his intrigues in various measures.

> Memmius and Ticida their songs did fill
>   With shameless themes and words I ne'er gave way to,
> So Cinna, Anser more lascivious still,
>   As well as Cornificius and Cato.

Poem XVII.

THE subject of this poem is January and May—a lethargic old fool wedded to a blooming young girl. Muretus thinks Verona is the town referred to; while Scaliger and Vossius contend for Novo Como.

CARM. XVII. v. 15.

Et puella tenellulo delicatior haedo.

Cf. Ovid. Met. xiii. 791— . . . tenero lascivior haedo.
And Theoc. Idyll. xi. 20, 21— '. . . ἁπαλωτέρα ἀρνός
Μόσχω γαυροτέρα.

POEMS XVIII., XIX., XX.

THE first of these poems is undoubtedly a fragment of a piece by Catullus. The authenticity of the other two is more than doubtful; but, as they appear in many editions of Catullus, it has been deemed advisable to give them in this translation.

CARM. XVIII. v. 2.

Qua domus tua Lampsaci est.

Cf. Priapeia, 76, 15—

Mortales tibi Lampsacum dicarunt.

Lampsacus was an important city of Mysia on the coast of the Hellespont. It was the chief seat of the worship of Priapus.

CARM. XIX. v. 6.

(1.) Pauperis tugurî pater, filiusque coloni.
(2.)   . . . . . tenellus.
(3.) Pauperis tugurî pater ipse filiolusque.

These are the conjectural emendations of Scaliger, Vossius, and Handius respectively. I have followed the last.

Cf. Virg. Eclog. i. 69.
> Pauperis et tuguri congestum cespite culmen.

V. 14.   Uva——umbra.

Cf. Virg. Eclog. vii. 58—
> Liber pampineas invidit collibus umbras.

V. 15, 16.
> Sanguine hanc etiam mihi (sed tacebitis) aram
> Barbatus linit hirculus.

Cf. Theoc. Epigr. i. 5—

> Βωμὸν δ' αἱμάξει κεραὸς τράγος οὗτος ὁ μᾶλος.

> The horn'd white he-goat shall thine altar stain.

CARM. XX. v. 6-9. Mihi——frigore.

Cf. Priapeia, lxxxiv.
> Vere rosa, autumno pomis, aestate frequentor
> Spicis: una mihi est horrida pestis hiems.
> Nam frigus metuo: et vereor, ne ligneus ignem
> Hac Deus ignaris praebeat agricolis.

> Spring brings me roses, summer ears of corn,
> Autumn rich fruits: in winter I'm forlorn.
> I fear not cold, but dread lest boors conspire
> To chop me into logs to feed the fire.

V. 13.

Cf. Virg. Eclog. i. 36—
> Non unquam gravis aere domum mihi dextra redibat.

And Moretum, v. 81—
> Inde domum cervice levis gravis aere redibat.

Poem XXII.

In these lines to Varus, Catullus ridicules the absurd conduct and inordinate vanity of Suffenus. This conceited scribbler, mentioned also in Carm. xiv. v. 19, is otherwise unknown.

CARM. XXII. v. 15–17.   ——neque——miratur.

Cf. Hor. Epist. ii. 2, 107, 108.

> Gaudent scribentes et se venerantur, et ultro,
> Si taceas, laudant quicquid scripsere, beati.

> They write, and with approving smile
> They idolise themselves the while,
> And praise—if you should silent sit—
> Their own blest lot and matchless wit.

V. 20.   Suus quoique attributus est error.

Cf. Propert. iii. 15, 13–20. (ii. 22, 13–20.)—

> Quaeris, Demophoon, cur sim tam mollis in omnes?
>   Quod quaeris Quare non habet ullus amor.
> Cur aliquis sacris laniat sua brachia cultris
>   Et Phrygis insanos caeditur ad numeros?
> *Unicuique dedit vitium natura creato:*
>   Mi fortuna aliquid semper amare dedit:
> Me licet et Thamyrae cantoris fata sequantur,
>   Nunquam ad formosas, invide, caecus ero.

> Why do I melt at every Beauty's charms?
>   Why ask me? such a "why" love never knew.
> Why with the knife does votary gash his arms,
>   And to the frantic notes his members hew?
>
> *Some failing nature did to each assign—*
>   My fate has ever been to love the fair;
> And, Envy! though rapt Thamyras' doom be mine,
>   I never will be blind if Beauty's there.

V. 21.
> Sed non videmus manticae quod in tergo est.

Cf. Phaedr. Fab. iv. 10. (Nisard's Collection)—
> Peras imposuit Jupiter nobis duas:
> Propriis repletam vitiis post tergum dedit,
> Alienis ante pectus suspendit gravem.
> Hac re videre nostra mala non possumus;
> Alii simul delinquunt, censores sumus.

> Two wallets Jove to each assign'd,
> Both fill'd with faults: the one behind
> Contains our own: the one before
> With others' sins is brimming o'er;
> Hence 'tis we cannot see our own,
> Our neighbours' in a trice are shown.

Cf. also Burns—
> O wad some power the giftie gie us
> *To see oursels as others see us.*

POEM XXIII.

IF this Furius is the person mentioned in poems xi. and xvi. he must have been in extreme poverty. Catullus could hardly have been expected to lend money to a man whose house could not boast of a fire, a spider, or a bug!

Cf. with this poem, *passim*, Mart. Epigr. xi. 32.

Poem XXIV.

Doering and others think that the "penniless beau" is Furius, to whom the preceding poem is addressed. Perhaps it is Aurelius. (Cf. Carm. xv. and xxi.)

Carm. XXIV. v. 7.

Qui? non est homo bellus? inquies. est.

A beau (*bellus homo*) is thus defined by Martial, (Epigr. iii. 63.)

> Cotile, bellus homo es: dicunt hoc, Cotile, multi.
>   Audio: sed quid sit, dic mihi, bellus homo?
> Bellus homo est, flexos qui digerit ordine crines:
>   Balsama qui semper, cinnama semper olet:
> Cantica qui Nili, qui Gaditana susurrat:
>   Qui movet in varios brachia volsa modos:
> Inter femineas tota qui luce cathedras
>   Desidet, atque aliqua semper in aure sonat:
> Qui legit hinc illinc missas, scribitque tabellas:
>   Pallia vicini qui refugit cubiti:
> Qui scit quam quis amet, qui per convivia currit:
>   Hirpini veteres qui bene novit avos.
> Quid narras? hoc est, hoc est homo, Cotile, bellus?
>   Res praetricosa est, Cotile, bellus homo.

> Cotilus, you are a beau; yes, Cotilus, many declare it.
>   Such is the story I hear: tell me, then, what is a beau?
> Why, sir, a beau is a man who arranges his tresses in order:
>   Smelling for ever of balm, smelling of cinnamon spice:
> Singing the songs of the Nile or a-humming the ditties of Cadiz:
>   Never at rest with his arms, moving them this way or that:
> Lounging on sofas from morning to night with a bevy of ladies:
>   Aye in the ears of some girl whispering some silly tale:

Reading a letter from Rhode or Chloe, or writing to Phyllis:
· Shunning the sleeve of his friend lest he should ruffle his dress:
Everyone's sweetheart he'll tell you, he swaggers the lion at parties:
Bets on the favourite horse, tells you his sire and his dam.
Cotilus, what are you telling me?—this thing! is this thing a beau?
Cotilus, then I must say he's a contemptible thing.

Poem XXV.

CARM. XXV. v. 1, 2.

   —— mollior cuniculi capillo
 `Vel anseris medullula.

Cf. Priapeia, lxiv. 1.

   Quidam, mollior anseris medulla.

V. 7.   Thynos.
Vide infra, Carm. xxxi.

Poem XXVI.

THE point of this poem lies in the first line, of which there is a double reading—some editors giving " nostra," others " vostra." We have followed the former, which has been adopted by Doering, Haupt, Rossbach, Ellis, &c.

Poem XXVII.

This little poem has the genuine Anacreontic ring. Catullus means a drinking-bout in earnest, and water is out of the question. It was customary, however, with the ancients to drink their wine diluted. Here is one recipe; nor are the perfumes and roses forgotten. (Mart. Epigr. v. 64.)

> Two-sixths of old Falèrn, Callistus, pour for me,
> Let summer snows be mix'd, young Alcimus, by thee,
> Around my shining locks diffuse the unguents free,
> And round my temples string sweet roses from the tree.
> Yon splendid tombs say: Grasp the moments ere they fly,
> For they declare that even gods themselves can die.

The same poet, in a charming little piece, recommends his friend Liber, unguented and rose-crowned, to indulge his genius with a beaker of old Falernian. (Epigr. viii. 77.)

> Liber, to all thy friends in close affection bound,
> O worthy thou to live with rose eternal crown'd:
> If thou art wise, thy locks with Syrian nard will shine,
> And ever round thy brow the rosy garlands twine;
> The old Falernian blacken aye thy crystal bowl,
> And o'er thy downy bed, Love, hovering, cheer thy soul.
> Who middle age hath seen, directing thus his ways,
> Hath far outlived, I ween, the measure of his days.

As we will not have another opportunity, for this is the only poem by Catullus in praise of wine, we may be pardoned for giving here the following tit-bit of Anacreon's philosophy, (xix.):—

> Black earth drinks the rain; the trees
>   Drain the earth again;
> Ocean quaffs the mountain breeze;
>   Phoebus swills the main;

Dian drinks the sun's bright beam ;
Then why blame ye me,
Friends, if I the red wine's stream
Quaff right joyously?

CARM. XXVII. v. 1, 2.

Minister vetuli, puer, Falerni,
Inger mi calices amariores.

Cf. Burns— Go fetch to me a pint o' wine,
An' fill it in a silver tassie.

And Tennyson, in "Will Waterproof's Lyrical Monologue"—
O plump head-waiter at the Cock,
To which I most resort,
How goes the time? 'Tis five o'clock.
Go fetch a pint of port:
But let it not be such as that
You set before chance-comers,
But such whose father-grape grew fat
On Lusitanian summers.

V. 5, 6. ————lymphae
Vini pernicies.

Propertius (iii. 31, 25-28) (ii. 33, 25-28) seems to consider "wine" the "bane of water:"—

Lenta bibis : mediae nequeunt te frangere noctes.
An nondum est talos mittere lassa manus?
Ah pereat, quicumque meracas repperit uvas
Corrupitque bonas nectare primus aquas !

Late, late thou drink'st; not midnight bids thee rise ;
And canst thou, tireless, still the dice endure ?
Curst be the man who grapeward cast his eyes,
And first with nectar spoil'd the water pure !

POEM XXVIII.

IN this piece of trenchant invective Catullus attacks Piso and his own praetor, Memmius, with all the bitterness of personal hate. Verannius and Fabullus, in their expedition, had been no more successful than our poet in his. He therefore dissuades them from a second trial of the service with the contemptuous sneer, " Pete nobiles amicos." In this poem we have a sample of the determined spirit in which Catullus was ever ready to assail autocracy. It was all one to him whether the despot was a Memmius or a Piso, a Mamurra or a Caesar.

POEM XXIX.

MAMURRA and Caesar are now the victims of the poet's lash. The former is doubtless the ostensible subject of attack, but he affords Catullus an excellent opportunity for attacking the " foremost man in all the world." Catullus cannot brook the idea that a charlatan and libertine like Mamurra should. drain and harass the countries of Gaul and Britain, nay, more, should be permitted to bring shame and dishonour to the very hearths and homes of the Roman people. He openly charges Mamurra with gross debauchery and reckless tyranny, and fearlessly taxes Caesar himself with infamous enormities.

It has been supposed, from a passage in Suetonius, that this poem, or the one numbered lvii., was read to Caesar when he visited Cicero at his Tusculan villa. Either of these poems, we should think, would have brought down on the head of the offender the signal vengeance of the Dictator. So far from that being the case, Suetonius informs us (Caes. cap. lxxxiii.) that Caesar not only forgave him on his apologising for his rashness, but continued to live on terms of intimacy with his father. If this statement is correct, Caesar must not only have stood in great awe of the bitter lampoons of Catullus, but must have considered leniency and forbearance as the best means of securing immunity from the virulence of his pen.

CARM. XXIX. v. 9.
Ut albulus columbus aut Adonëus.

This is the common reading, but it is manifestly corrupt, there being no such word as Adonëus.

The reading of Muretus and Heinsius is better, though still objectionable—
Ut albulus columbulus Dīōnēus.

Schwabius reads—
Ut albulus columbus haut idóneus,
which, though quite satisfactory in respect of quantity, appears forced and frigid.

Why not
Ut albulus columbus aut Ionicus,
(or Ionius)?

Cf. Plaut. Stich. 750—
Qui Ionicus aut cinaedicus, qui hoc tale facere possiet?

And Hor. Od. iii. 6, 21, 22—
Motus doceri gaudet Ionicos
Matura virgo.

On the amorous nature of the pigeon, *vide* Catull. lxviii. 125 - 128; and parallels to the same passage, *infra*.

POEM XXX.

This poem is full of grief and tender pathos. In what circumstances Alphenus (Varus?) had proved false to the poet and broken the sacred ties of friendship we have no means of ascertaining. It is quite evident, however, that he had been on terms of the closest intimacy and friendship with Catullus, else he would not have thus deplored his perfidy. This piece is very different in tone from those in which he denounces the disgraceful conduct of Furius, Aurelius, and others who had enjoyed his friendship.

CARM. XXX. v. 4. Nec——placent.
Cf. Hom. Odyss. xiv. 83—

Οὐ μὲν σχέτλια ἔργα θεοὶ μάκαρες φιλέουσιν.

―――◆―――

POEM XXXI.

This lovely little poem appears to have been written by Catullus immediately after his return from Bithynia. Emancipated from the thrall of Memmius, and travelsore from a fruitless expedition to a barbaric land, he is enraptured at the sight of his beloved Sirmio, and gives vent to his joyous feelings with all the fervour of a boy.

Sirmio (*Sirmione*) is connected with the mainland by a long and narrow bank, and has almost the appearance of an island. It is little more than two miles in circumference, and lies in the bosom of Lake Benacus (*Lago di*

Garda), whose sea-green waters, though smiling so sweetly for Catullus, did sometimes wear a frown : (Virg. Georg. ii. 160)—

Fluctibus et fremitu adsurgens, Benace, marino.

The peninsula is fringed with rows of cypress trees ; and somewhere along its shore was the quiet cove in which Catullus stowed the yacht that brought him safely home from his wanderings. (*Vide* Carm. iv.)

The site of what must have been a splendid villa—700 feet long by 300 broad—which many conceive to have been the patrimonial mansion of the poet, may still be seen. If, as Vulpius thinks from the word "*herus*" in the poem, the whole peninsula belonged to him, he must have been in princely circumstances, and all his outcries against poverty must be treated as a joke.

Napoleon, in 1797, on his way to sign the treaty of Campo Formio, turned aside to visit the site of the poet's residence. Two years afterwards the French general-in-chief La Combe St Michel visited it, got it surveyed, and caused a ground-plan to be taken.* The general gave a splendid fête in honour of the ancient poet-lord of Sirmio, whose praises were sung on the occasion by the Italian bard Anelli.

The Lacus Benacus is in extent about forty miles by ten. Why it is called the Lydian Lake by Catullus is not quite apparent. Some commentators explain it thus: It lay in the Veronese territory which belonged to the Rhaeti, the Rhaeti sprang from the Tuscans, the Tuscans from the Lydians. Rossbach repudiates this view, and considers the line corrupt.

---

* More recent investigations tend to show that this villa does not belong to the period of Catullus. but rather to that of the Emperor Constantine. *Vide* Schwabii Quaest. Catull. p. 51.

CARM. XXXI. v. 4.
Quam te libenter quamque laetus inviso.
Cf. Anal. Vet. Poet. Gr. Brunkii. T. iii. Carm. xviii. p. 146—
Χαῖρ' Ἰθάκη, μετ' ἄεθλα, μετ' ἄλγεα πικρὰ θαλάσσης
Ἀσπασίως τεὸν οὖδας ἱκάνομαι.

Hail Ithaca! from grievous woe and toil
Endured by sea, I gladly hail thy soil.

V. 5.   ——Thyniam atque Bithynos.

Bithynia was possessed at an early period by two Thracian tribes, called Thyni and Bithyni. The former dwelt on the coast, the latter in the interior.

V. 9.   ——fessi venimus larem ad nostrum,
Desideratoque acquiescimus lecto.

Cf. Tibull. i. 1, 43, 44—
—————— satis est, requiescere lecto
Sei licet et solito membra levare toro.

Enough: reclining on my couch to rest
And stretch my limbs upon the accustomed bed.

———◆———

POEM XXXII.

Cf. with this piece, *passim*, Ovid. Amor. I. El. v.

V. 7, 8.   ————paresque nobis
novem &c.

Cf. Ovid. Amor. iii. 7, 25, 26—
Exigere a nobis angusta nocte Corinnam,
Me memini numeros sustinuisse novem.

V. 11.   Pertundo &c.

Cf. Mart. Epigr. xi. 16, 5—
O quoties rigida pulsabis pallia vena!

Poem XXXIV.

This poem, which Scaliger tried to identify with the hymn sung at the Secular Festival, A.U.C. 737, is neither more nor less than a hymn in praise of Diana. Catullus had died long before that time, and it is hardly likely that he wrote the poem for posterity. Besides, the secular hymn in honour of Apollo and Diana was sung in alternate stanzas or parts by a chorus of youths and maidens; whereas here both sing the same words. Moreover, there is no allusion to Apollo in the poem. It is merely, as we have said, a hymn to Diana, praying for the prosperity of the Roman people. In the fifth stanza allusion is made to the moon borrowing her light from the sun—a fact well known to the ancients, as witness Lucian "De Astrologia," and Pliny, ii. 9.

Cf. Hor. Od. i. 21, and iii. 22, in both of which he has borrowed from this poem of Catullus.

Poem XXXV.

This little poem affords us a pleasing example of the amenity in which Catullus lived with his worthy brethren of the lyre. Caecilius, as appears from this piece, had written a poem on Cybele, from which circumstance some have gone so far as to assign to him the authorship of "Atys." On what grounds this conclusion is reached we are at a loss to discover, as Atys, not Cybele, is the subject of the poem by Catullus. The song of Caecilius that so enchanted the young lady here referred to has perished; and so likewise would the name of the author but for this friendly epistle. Caecilius resided at *New Como*, a town on the Lacus Larius seu Comacenus (Lago di Como).

The extreme length of the Lacus Larius is about fifty miles; its extreme breadth not more than eight.

———◆———

Poem XXXVI.

THE Volusius of this poem and the 95th is probably Tanusius Geminus, a silly and voluminous annalist mentioned by Seneca in one of his Epistles. *Vide* Schwabii Quaest. Catull. p. 279, *seqq.*

CARM. XXXVI. v. 6-8.

    Electissima ——— lignis.

Cf. Tibull. i. 9, 47-50—

  Quin etiam attonita laudes tibi mente canebam,
   Et me nunc nostri Pieridumque pudet.
  Illa velim rapida Vulcanus carmina flamma
   Torreat et liquida deleat amnis aqua.

  Struck with thy charms my muse enshrined thy name:
   I'm now ashamed I ever sang thy praise.
  May Vulcan burn with swift-devouring flame
   And rushing streams obliterate my lays.

V. 12-14. Quae ——— Golgos.

Cf. Virg. Aen. x. 51—

  Est Amathus, est celsa mihi Paphos, atque Cythera,
   Idaliaeque domus.

———◆———

Poem XXXVII.

The poet vents his indignation against a number of dissolute youths who had seduced the object of his affections. Chief among these was Egnatius, a long-haired, black-bearded fop, (*vide* Carm. xxxix.) Their place of meeting was a low tavern a few doors from the temple of Castor and Pollux.

These gods, here called *fratres pileati* from the circumstance of their wearing conical caps, were worshipped as the "Penates populi Romani." Their temple stood on the south side of the Forum, beside a fountain called the *Lacus Juturnae*, at which they watered their steeds after the battle of Lake Regillus, (B.C. 496). It was dedicated B.C. 484, on the ides of Quintilis, the anniversary of the battle.

Poem XXXVIII.

Catullus, prostrated by some great grief, upbraids Cornificius for forsaking him in the hour of his distress. This friend is considered by some to be the poet mentioned by Ovid in the line, (Trist. ii. 436)—

>   Et leve Cornifici parque Catonis opus.

Excursus I.
Carm. XXXVIII. verse 8.

Simonides.

Simonides, the most celebrated elegiac poet of Greece, was a native of Ceos, an island in the Aegean. He was born about the year 556 B.C., and, after an honoured life spent in his native island, and afterwards successively at Athens, Sparta, and Syracuse, died at the advanced age of ninety. The attentions paid to him by Hipparchus at Athens, Pausanias at Lacedemon, and Hiero at Syracuse, attest the high estimation in which he was held by the magnates of his time. The people of Syracuse showed him a degree of honour rarely accorded to poets in their lifetime, and after his death erected a splendid monument to his memory.

His compositions, which excelled in sweetness (whence his surname *Melicertes*), combined, with the most tender pathos, the rarest poetic conception and harmony of expression. Though he was inferior in originality and passionate intensity to some of his predecessors and contemporaries, his lays were esteemed by Hiero more than the matchless odes of Pindar or the dignified strains of Bacchylides.

His works, which included dramatic, elegiac, epigrammatic, and lyrical pieces—now for the most part lost—were written in the Doric dialect.

Simonides was the inventor of the new elegy (ἔλεγος), the "*querimonia*" of Horace, as distinguished from the old martial poem (ἐλεγεῖον), also written in distichs of alternate hexameters and pentameters, whose origin is attributed to Callinus (B.C. 776).

POEM XXXIX.

CATULLUS ridicules the silly and offensive behaviour of Egnatius, who, from Carm. xxxvii. *ante*, would seem to have been a successful rival in some love affair. Egnatius was a native of Celtiberia, a district in the high tableland in the centre of Spain. Its inhabitants, as the name implies, were a mixed people of Celts and Spaniards (Celtae et Iberi). They had recourse to a most singular cosmetic for the purpose of beautifying their skin and imparting a snowy whiteness to their teeth. In the lines

. . . Celtiberia in terra,
Quod quisque minxit, hoc solet sibi mane
Dentem atque russam defricare gingivam,

Catullus is guilty of no exaggeration, for Diodorus Siculus (Book V.), when speaking of the Celtiberians, bears testimony to the custom—

τὸ σῶμα λούουσι οὔρῳ καὶ τοὺς ὀδόντας.

CARM. XXXIX. v. 16.

Nam risu inepto res ineptior nulla est.

Cf. Poet. Gr. Gnom. v. 83, 84, p. 224. Edit. Brunck.

Γέλως ἄκαιρος ἐν βροτοῖς δεινὸν κακόν.
Γελᾷ δ' ὁ μῶρος, κἄν τι μὴ γελοῖον ᾖ.

———◆———

POEM XL.

THOUGH Catullus has left no laboured peroration to his works like Horace and Ovid, he seems from this, and several other poems, to have been equally certain of the immortality of his productions. He cannot understand why Ravidus, Aurelius, Gellius, &c., should be foolish enough to pursue a course which will be certain to secure for them an eternity of infamy.

———◆———

POEM XLI.

CATULLUS in this poem and the 43d lampoons the mistress of Mamurra. From the portrait which he has drawn of her she certainly must have been a very hag; yet it is more than likely that it was in great measure owing to the utter detestation in which he held Mamurra himself that these poems were written.

Mamurra was a Roman knight, born at Formiae, who followed the fortunes of Caesar in Gaul as commander of engineers (*praefectus fabrûm*), in which capacity he managed, by dint of unscrupulous conduct and inveterate tyranny, to amass a princely fortune, which he as recklessly squandered. Hence the epithet "*decoctor*," applied to him in the poem.

He built a palatial residence on the Coelian Hill, and was the first man in Rome, according to Pliny, who incrusted his walls with marble, and ornamented the structure with solid pillars of the same.

———◆———

POEM XLII.

HENDECASYLLABIC verse, with Catullus, was alike suited to tender playfulness, voluptuous passion, and bitter invective.

It was the vehicle of his feelings in the charming poems on the sparrow, in the burning kissing-songs to Lesbia, and in many occasional pieces, whether written in frolic, indignation, or hate.

Of 116 poems which remain to us of his writings, no fewer than thirty-nine are in this metre. It is sometimes called "Phalaecian," from Phalaecus, its inventor.

CARM. XLII. v. 8.   Turpe incedere.

The ancients set a high value on an easy, graceful step. *Vide* Ovid. A.A. iii. 297-300 —

Omnibus his, quoniam prosunt, impendite curam.
　Discite femineo corpora ferre gradu.
Est et in incessu pars non contempta decoris:
　Allicit ignotos ille fugatque viros.

For what they're worth, these precepts duly prize:
　A graceful walk and carriage still maintain;
In woman's step no mean attraction lies,
　And it may banish or allure a swain.

POEM XLIII.

Cf. this poem *passim* with xli.

V. 1.　　Salve, nec minimo puella naso,
　　　　Nec bello pede, &c.

Contrast with this description the lines of Propertius (ii. 2, 5-8.)

Fulva coma est longaeque manus, et maxima toto
　Corpore, et incedit vel Jove digna soror,
Aut cum Dulichias Pallas spatiatur ad aras,
　Gorgonis anguiferae pectus operta comis.

Flaxen her hair, hands slender, form divine;
　No queenlier aspect Juno's self could wear,
Or Pallas walking by Dulichian shrine,
　With breast conceal'd by Gorgon's snaky hair.

POEM XLIV.

THIS villa seems to have been situated on the very boundary line of Sabinum and Latium. Hence it could be said with almost equal propriety to lie in either one or other of these districts. It must have been in the immediate vicinity of Tibur, and, doubtless, from the exceeding amenity of the latter place, Catullus was anxious that his villa should be associated with it, at least in name.

Horace, too, though possessing a farm in Sabinum, equal to all his wants and desires, was nevertheless constrained to breathe a wish that Tibur might one day become the home of his old age, (Od. II. 6, 5-8)—

> Tibur, Argeo positum colono,
> Sit meae sedes utinam senectae;
> Sit modus lasso maris et viarum
> > Militiaeque.

Its great natural beauty; the wild, rushing Anio on which it stood; the vine and olive groves around it; the ancient temples in its vicinity; and the society of the choicest spirits of the age, gave it a charm in his eyes beyond all other places, (Od. II. 6, 14, 15)—

> Ille terrarum mihi praeter omnes
> Angulus ridet.

It was here that, with the industry of a bee, he fashioned many of those wonderful poems which have been the delight and admiration of every succeeding age.

(Od. IV. 2, 27-32.) ——ego, apis Matinae
> More modoque,
> Grata carpentis thyma per laborem
> Plurimum, circa nemus uvidique
> Tiburis ripas, operosa parvus
> > Carmina fingo.

———◆———

POEM XLV.

THIS is one of the most charming songs of antiquity. It is such a one as Catullus might have written and sung to Lesbia ere a doubt had arisen in his heart "to dim the purple light of love."

CARM. XLV. v. 8.
> Hoc ut dixit, Amor, sinistram ut ante,
> Dextram sternuit approbationem.

This is the common reading, but surely *sinistra approbatio* sounds very like nonsense.

The reading given by Rossbach is, besides being free from objection, far more intelligible—

> Hoc ut dixit, Amor sinistrâ, ut ante,
> Dextram sternuit approbationem,

that is, "Amor ut ante fecerat, a sinistrâ ad dextram sternuit, quae fuit dextra approbatio vel omen secundum."

Cf. with this couplet Propert. ii. 3, 23–26—

> Num tibi nascenti primis, mea vita, diebus
> Candidus argutum sternuit omen Amor?
> Haec tibi contulerunt caelestia munera divi,
> Haec tibi ne matrem forte dedisse putes.

> My life! O tell me, at thy natal hour
> Did radiant Love a clear, bright omen sneeze?
> Such charms as thine were Heaven's all priceless dower:
> Think not thy mother gave thee gifts like these.

Theoc. Idyll. vii. 95—

> Σιμιχίδᾳ μεν Ἔρωτες ἐπέπταρον.

And Hom. Odyss. xvii. 545—

> Οὐχ ὁράᾳσ ὅ μοι υἱὸς ἐπέπταρε πᾶσιν ἔπεσσιν.

V. 11–16.   Sic——medullis.

Nott, Lamb, and Martin seem to have entirely misunderstood the meaning of this passage. So far as we can see, there is no comparison instituted between the love of Septimius and that of Acme. The meaning is: Let me love thee with a devotion increasing with the ever-increasing ardour of my affection; nothing more.

V. 20.   Mutuis animis amant amantur.

Cf. Chaucer, in the "Knightes Tale,"—
> For now is Palamon in al his wele
> Lyvynge in blisse, richesse and in hele,
> And Emelye him loveth so tendirly,
> And he hir serveth al so gentilly,
> That never was ther wordes hem betweene
> Of jealousy ne of non other tene.

POEM XLVI.

THESE lines are redolent of the warmth and freshness of a spring morning. The rigours of winter are past; the storms that attend the equinox—coeli furor aequinoctialis—have ceased to rave; the west wind is blowing gently; the scorching sun is beginning to be felt on the broad flat plains of Nicaea: Catullus must away. He is in an ecstasy of joy at the prospect of leaving Bithynia and visiting the renowned cities of Asia.

The tone of the last three lines is indicative of the warm affection which Catullus ever cherished for a worthy object.

POEM XLVII.

CATULLUS is ever ready to vent his ire against Piso and all his belongings. This poem, of little or no consequence in itself, is especially valuable as proving beyond a doubt that Cn. Calpurnius Piso, mentioned by Sallust,

(Cat. cap. xix., &c.) was not the praetor in whose suite Verannius and Fabullus went to Spain. Cn. Calpurnius Piso, we know from Sallust, was killed when making a progress through his province. This Piso, we learn from the poem before us, actually returned with his ill-gotten gains and continued to sumptuously feast and entertain two of his minions, Porcius and Socration; while he entirely discarded the two friends of Catullus.

Poem XLVIII.

Vide vii. and notes, *supra*.

Poem XLIX.

THE circumstances in which these complimentary lines were addressed to the prince of Roman orators are entirely unknown to us. It appears certain, however, that the poet had been indebted to him for some service in which his oratorical powers had been called into play. Viewing these 'lines dispassionately, we see no grounds for thinking that Catullus lived on terms of intimacy with Cicero, as almost every editor and chance biographer he has found would have us believe. They have nothing of the careless *abandon* or genial ring which we find in his poems to his intimate friends. They indicate the highest appreciation of the orator's talent and abilities, and breathe the feeling of gratitude: nothing more.

POEM L.

THIS effusion, dashed off during a sleepless night, after a day of festive merriment, is in the poet's happiest vein.

For notices of Licinius, see note to Carm. XIV. and Excursus to Carm. LIII.

―――◆―――

POEM LI.*

THIS is a vigorous translation of a portion of Sappho's famous ode (Πρὸς γυναῖκα ἐρωμένην) preserved by Longinus.

If Catullus translated the last stanza, his version of it has perished.

CARM. LI.

Cf. with this poem, *passim*, the conclusion of Tennyson's "Eleänore"—

> I watch thy grace; and in its place
> My heart a charmèd slumber keeps,
>   While I muse upon thy face;
> And a languid fire creeps
>   Through my veins to all my frame,
> Dissolvingly and slowly: soon
> From thy rose-red lips my name
> Floweth; and then, as in a swoon,
>   With dinning sound my ears are rife,
>   My tremulous tongue faltereth,
>   I lose my colour, I lose my breath,
>   I drink the cup of a costly death,
> Brimmed with delirious draughts of warmest life.
>   I die with my delight, before
>   I hear what I would hear from thee;
>   Yet tell thy name again to me,
>   I *would* be dying evermore,
>   So dying ever, Eleänore.

Excursus II.

CARM. LI.ᵇ

Otium, Catulle, tibi molestum est :
Otio exultas nimiumque gestis.
Otium et reges prius et beatas
  Perdidit urbes.

This stanza is generally printed as part of the preceding poem. With regard to its merits and aptness as a conclusion to a translation of Sappho's ode, different opinions are entertained. Doering considers it quite in keeping with the rest of the poem, and adduces what he considers a parallel instance from Ovid (Rem. Amor. 135-151). The lines of Ovid, however, form part of an original poem ; these appear as the conclusion of a translation.

But it is to one of his French biographers, l'Abbé Arnaud, that we must go for a superlative estimate of this stanza. We give his translation of the ode in question and remarks entire:—

" ' Celui-là me paraît égaler, et, s'il est possible, surpasser les dieux en bonheur, qui jouit de ta présence, de ton entretien et de ton sourire. Quant à moi, j'en ai perdu l'usage de tous mes sens. Au moment même où je t'ai vue, ô Lesbie, je n'ai pu retrouver la parole ; ma langue est demeurée immobile ; un feu subtil a parcouru tout mon corps ; un bruit soudain s'est formé dans mes oreilles, et mes yeux se sont couverts de ténèbres.' Quand tout à coup, honteux de sa situation, qu'il devait sans doute à une vie molle et désœuvrée, il ajoute : 'Catulle, tu vois combien l'oisiveté t'est funeste, et tu t'y plais, et tu l'aimes ! l'oisiveté cependant a perdu les plus grands monarques et les plus florissants empires.' Je ne sais si je me trompe, mais cette réflexion soudaine, à la suite du délire de la passion me semble admirable ; c'est un rayon qui, au moment où l'on s'y attend le moins, perce le nuage et promet de le dissiper ; d'ailleurs ce mouvement me paraît tout à fait selon la nature, qui, en accordant à l'homme une excessive sensibilité, a voulu le distinguer de tous les autres êtres sensibles par l'inestimable présent de la raison et du pouvoir de la faire régner sur les actions et sur les pensées."

The Abbé, it will be seen, considers the reflection admirable in the place which it occupies; but, notwithstanding his eloquent defence of it, we fail to see its appropriateness. We have no fault to find with the *reflection*. Indeed, it might have been better for the fame of Catullus had he oftener moralised in this way. But, surely, this was not the place for such a thing. The stanza, moreover, is poor at best, and we should be sorry to think that Catullus was capable of appending such a piece of bathos to Sappho's glorious ode.

It *may* be a fragment of a poem by Catullus, but most probably it is the work of some pedantic transcriber. The most cursory reader will see its value at once.

CARM. LI.[b]

Cf. Ovid. Rem. Amor. 135-144—

> Ergo ubi visus eris nostrae medicabilis arti,
>   Fac monitis fugias otia prima meis.
> Haec, ut ames, faciunt; haec quod fecere, tuentur:
>   Haec sunt jucundi causa cibusque mali.
> Otia si tollas, periere Cupidinis arcus,
>   Contemtaeque jacent et sine luce faces.
> Quam platanus vino gaudet, quam populus unda,
>   Et quam limosa canna palustris humo,
> Tam Venus otia amat. Qui finem quaeris amoris—
>   Cedit amor rebus—res age, tutus eris.

Ease genders love and fosters it when born,
Alike the cause and food of life's sweet thorn;
Dispel it, Cupid's shafts no longer fly;
Extinguished and despised his torches lie.
As vines the plane, as streams the poplar please,
As miry ground the reed, even so doth ease
Glad love. Then, if a love-sick heart thou 'dst cure—
Love yields to toil—toil hard and thou 'rt secure.

ILLUSTRATIVE NOTES. 227

POEM LII.

THIS quartette, if not the latest of the poems of Catullus, contains at least distinct mention of events later than any alluded to in his extant works. Vatinius held the consulship along with Quintus Fusius Calenus, A.U.C. 707, (see Excursus to Carm. LIII.) Catullus, if we are right in assuming A.U.C. 678 as the date of his birth, would at this time be about thirty years of age.

———◆———

EXCURSUS III.

CARM. LIII.

Dii magni, salaputium disertum!—(Verse 5.)

The rhetorical powers of little Calvus—erat enim parvulus statura—were on this occasion exerted against Publius Vatinius, one of the most notorious villains and miscreants, according to Cicero, that ever cumbered the soil of any country. Starting in life as a political adventurer, Vatinius became quaestor B.C. 63, and tribune of the plebs B.C. 59. In the latter year he became the bought servant of Caesar, and afterwards witnessed against Milo and Sestius B.C. 56, a circumstance that called forth from Cicero, in a speech yet extant, one of the most severe castigations ever inflicted. He obtained the praetorship B.C. 55, and in the following year was accused of corruption by Calvus in the speech referred to in this poem. On this occasion he was defended by Cicero, a fact which does not redound very highly to the honour of that orator after his former oration.

We are told by Seneca (Controv. III. cap. 19) that Calvus was so vehement in this impeachment, that Vatinius interrupted him and said to the judges: "Rogo vos, judices, si iste disertus est, ideo me damnari oportet?" (I pray you, judges, because that man is eloquent, does it follow that I must be condemned?)

As an orator Calvus attained a high reputation. He was a most accurate speaker, and his compositions evinced great taste, delicacy, and polish. (Cic. de Clar. Orat. S. 283.)

Quintilian tells us that some preferred him to all the orators of his time, while others were of opinion that he weakened his productions by combing them with a too unsparing hand. To imitate successfully the Attic orators was the highest aim of his ambition. (Quint. lib. x. 1.)

Tacitus, in his dialogue concerning oratory (Sect. xxxiv.), speaks of the oration against Vatinius, which Calvus made at the age of twenty-seven, in terms of the highest praise. Calvus was born B.C. 82, and died at the early age of thirty-five or thirty-six (B.C. 47 or 46).

POEM LIV.

THIS invective against Caesar, which Muretus considered intelligible only to a Sybil, has been invested with a considerable degree of point and meaning by Doering. It is still, however, far from being an elegant production.

Rossbach, perhaps correctly, considers the lines fragments of two distinct poems.

POEM LV.

OF Camerius nothing is known.

CARM. LV.

Cf. with this poem, *passim*, Plaut. Amph. iv. 1, 1-6—
Naucratem quem convenire volui in navi non erat :
Neque domi, neque in urbe invenio quemquam, qui illum viderit.
Nam omneis plateas perreptavi, gymnasia et myropolia :

Apud emporium, atque in macello, in palaestra atque in foro :
In medicinis, in tonstrinis, apud omneis aedeis sacras,
Sum defessus quaeritando, nusquam invenio Naucratem.

I'm seeking Naucrates : I've tried the ship ; he is not there.
At home, in town I've found no one who's seen him anywhere;
The streets, gymnasia, nard-shops all, I've paced with weary foot,
The emporium, meat-shops, wrestling-ground, and market-place to boot,
I've been through druggists', barbers' shops, and all the temples round :
I'm tired with searching : Naucrates is nowhere to be found.

V. 18, 19.   Si linguam clauso tenes in ore,
             Fructus projicies amoris omnes.

Cf. Tibull. iv. 7, 1, 2—
    Tandem venit amor, qualem texisse pudori,
        Quam nudasse alicui sit mihi fama magis.

    Comes love at length, and, sooth, the honour's more
    To tell my flame, than, blushing, cloak it o'er.

POEM LVI.

THESE lines are probably addressed to Valerius Cato, poet and grammarian, (died B.C. 20).

POEM LVII.

FOR Caesar and Mamurra, see note to Carm. xxix., *supra*.

Poem LVIII.

"Last scene of all
That ends this strange eventful history."

Carm. LVIII. v. 4.

Nunc in quadriviis et angiportis.

Cf. Hor. Od. i. 25, 10—

Flebis in solo levis angiportu.

Carm. LIX. v. 3, 4.

Vidistis———panem.

Cf. Ter. Eun. iii. 2, 38—

E flamma petere te cibum posse arbitror.

Carm. LX.

Cf. with this fragment, *passim*, Carm. lxiv. 154-156, and parallel reference cited in the notes.

Poem LXI.

AFTER the lapse of nearly two thousand years, not only does this hymn retain all its pristine vigour and freshness, but it still stands unrivalled in the domain of erotic poetry. The number of lively images presented to the reader is truly marvellous ; not less so are the splendour of the diction and the harmony of the numbers. Highly sensuous in expression, redolent of voluptuous feeling, warm as the blushes of the bride, and evincing throughout the liveliest friendship for the bridegroom, it approaches nearer to perfection than any work of its class, whether of ancient or modern times. The English language, it is true, possesses one, which, if not so perfect as a work of art, is certainly transfused with a purer feeling and a nobler spirit. In this respect, however, they cannot be judged from the same point of view, inasmuch as that of Spenser is the production of a Christian poet.

Excursus IV.

NUPTIAL SONGS AND NUPTIAL CEREMONIES.

CARM. LXI.

The nuptial songs of the ancients were, strictly speaking, of three distinct kinds.

The first comprehended such as detailed the nuptial procession, pomp, and rites, and the relative duties of the bridegroom and bride. In these the praises of the happy pair were sung and hearty wishes expressed for their happiness. Sometimes there was a contest between a chorus of youths and maidens, (as in the following poem), the youths arguing strongly for, and the maidens as strongly against, matrimony. Such a poem, however, only related to what took place prior to the consummation of the nuptial ceremony, and was called among the Greeks *Hymenaeus*, and among the Romans *Thalassio*. To this class, in one or other of its forms, belong all the nuptial songs of Catullus.

Of the second kind was the epithalamium, properly so called, (ἐπιθαλάμιον κοιμητικόν), which was sung outside the bridal chamber after the bride and bridegroom had retired thither. Such, for example, is the 18th Idyllium of Theocritus, in which twelve Spartan virgins sing the praises of Menelaus and Helen.

The third kind was sung on the morning following the nuptials, and was called the "matin chaunt" (ἐπιθαλάμιον ἐγερτικόν). No specimen of this song has reached modern times.

It would be quite foreign to our purpose to give a minute and detailed account of the nuptial ceremonies of the Greeks and Romans, but a few remarks explanatory of the poem under consideration, and illustrative of the customs and rites therein alluded to, may not be altogether impertinent.

The tutelary god of marriage was Hymenaeus, and his name, in one formula ór other, was the principal burden in all nuptial songs. The origin of his name is differently accounted for, some deriving it from one Hymenaeus of Argos, who had generously rescued some Athenian virgins from the hands of the Pelasgi; some from the bridegroom and bride dwelling together (ἀπὸ 'τοῦ ὁμοῦ ναίειν), and others, perhaps correctly, from ὑμήν (*membrana*).

The Roman word Thalassius or Thalassio, which occurs frequently in nuptial songs, is said to be as old as the time of Romulus. We are told by Livy, that, when a virgin was being taken along at the time of the rape of the Sabine women, her safety was ensured and the way cleared for her on her captors crying out Thalassio (*for Thalassius*). This personage was a senator, and, from the above mentioned circumstance, his name came to be intimately associated with the leading home of the bride.

In this poem, Hymen, the patron of virtuous affection, is summoned from the Heliconian hill to escort the bride to the arms of the bridegroom, arrayed in the *Flammeum*, his locks crowned with flowers of marjoram, yellow sandals on his feet, and a pine-torch in his uplifted hand.

The bride was invariably attired in an under garment (*Regilla or Tunica recta*), which was girt round her with a woollen girdle (*Cingulum factum ex lana ovis*). A yellow net (*Reticulum luteum*) confined her tresses, which were parted either with a spear or an instrument of that form (*Hasta celibaris*). Over her head and face she wore a flame-coloured veil (*Flammeum*), large enough to reach the ground, and on her feet were yellow slippers (*Socci lutei*).

As she was conducted, thus attired, from her father's house to that of her betrothed, the nuptial song (*Hymenaeus*) was sung by her friends, who accompanied the words with the music of flutes (*Tibiae*). She was attended by three boys, two of whom acted as her supporters, the other preceded her carrying a hawthorn torch (*Spina alba*). Another youth (*Camillus*) carried a basket containing the industrial implements of a Roman matron—distaff, spindle, &c. When the bride reached the vestibule of her future home, she wreathed the door-posts with fillets of sacred wool, and anointed them with oil or lard, after which she was carefully lifted over the threshold, lest by any chance she should make an ill-omened stumble. On entering she saluted the bridegroom with the words *Ubi tu Caius ego Caia*. She was then presented by him with fire and water, in token that all the necessaries of life should thenceforward be shared by them in common.

The guests then partook of the banquet (*Coena nuptialis*), at the close of which nuts were scattered by the bridegroom as a proof that he had now relinquished the sports of his youth, and would henceforth act with the dignity becoming a married man. The banquet ended, the bride was escorted to the nuptial couch (*Lectus genialis*) by *Pronubae*, bridesmatrons, who differed from the bridesmaids of modern times only in the respect that they were married ladies who had been united to only one husband (*Univirae*). When the pair had retired to the nuptial chamber (*Thalamus*), a chorus of maidens sang the epithalamium. On the following day the bride offered sacrifice on the domestic altar, and in the afternoon the bridegoom gave an entertainment (*Repotia*), which concluded the ceremonies.

CARM. LXI.

Compare this poem, *passim*, with the nuptial songs of Solomon, of Spenser, and of Tennyson, also, in passages, with Chaucer's " Boke of the Duchesse."

V. 11-15.

Cf. Claudian Epith. Hon. et Mar.—

> Age, cuncta nuptiali
> Redimita vere tellus

>   Celebra toros heriles:
>   Omne nemus cum fluviis,
>   Omne canat profundum.

>   Let all the earth be gay,
>   And, clothed with flowers of spring,
>   Loud raise the nuptial lay
>   In honour of its king:
>   Let woods and streams to-day,
>   And seas with gladness sing.

V. 16-20.

Cf. Tibull. i. v. 43-46—
>   Non facit hoc verbis, facie tenerisque lacertis
>   Devovet et flavis nostra puella comis.
>   Talis ad Haemonium Nereis Pelea quondam
>   Vecta est fraenato caerula pisce Thetis.

>   With spells? no!—with fair shoulders, queenly charms,
>   And golden locks she lit this witching flame:
>   Lovely as to Haemonian Peleus' arms
>   On bridled fish blue Nereid Thetis came.

V. 34, 35.

Cf. Shakspeare, "Midsummer Night's Dream," Titania to Bottom—
>   ———the female ivy so
>   Enrings the barky fingers of the elm.

V. 56, *seqq.*

Cf. Claudian, Epith. Pallad. et Celer. 124, *seqq.*—
>   Aggreditur Cytherea nurum, flentemque pudico
>   Detraxit matris gremio: matura tumescit
>   Virginitas, superatque nives ac lilia candor,
>   Et patrium flavis testatur crinibus Istrum.
>   Tum dextram complexa viri, dextramque puellae
>   Tradit, et his ultro sancit connubia dictis:
>   "Vivite concordes, et nostrum discite munus."

> Then Cytherea bears away
>   The weeping maid, whose pleading arms
> Cling to her modest mother's breast,
> And well, I ween, her looks attest
>   The ripeness of her charms.
>
> The radiant whiteness of her face
>   Outvies the lily and the snow,
> Her golden tresses plainly say
> That she beheld her natal day
>   Where Ister's waters flow.
>
> And now she joins the lovers' hands,
>   Sheds on them both a smile benign,
> And with these words she seals the bond :
> "Live, love, be yours a union fond,
>   Enjoy what gifts are mine."

V. 61-75.

Cf. Claudian, same poem, 31-33—

> Hunc Musa genitum legit Cytherea, ducemque
> Praefecit thalamis: nullum junxisse cubile
> Hoc sine, nec primas fas est attollere taedas.

> Venus chose the Muse's son
>   O'er nuptial rites to reign supreme,
> And but for him no bridal bed
> Is blest: no brandished torches shed
>   Their hymenaeal gleam.

V. 79. Sed moraris: abit dies.

Cf. Calpurn. Eclog. v. 120, 121—

> Sed jam sera dies cadit, et jam, sole fugato,
> Frigidus aestivas impellit Noctifer horas.

Now pales the waning day, the sun is set,
And eve's cool star impels the scorching hours.

V. 114-119.   O cubile——Gaudeat.

Cf. Propert. iii. 7, 1, 2, (ii. 15, 1, 2.)—

    O me felicem! O nox mihi candida, et O tu
    Lectule, deliciis facte beate meis!

    O happy I! O loveliest night of nights!
    And thou, O bed, made blest by my delights!

V. 117, 118.   —— quae vaga Nocte.

Vaga is an epithet applied by the poets to anything that is borne along with perpetual motion (Doering). It is here, perhaps, merely ornamental (*epitheton ornans*). But Nox had a chariot as well as Sol, Luna, &c., and in this view it is peculiarly appropriate.

Cf. Theocr. Idyll. ii. 163-166—

    Ἀλλὰ τὺ μὲν χαίροισα ποτ' ὠκεανὸν τρέπε πώλως,
    Πότνι'· ἐγὼ δ' οἰσῶ τὸν ἐμὸν πόνον ὥσπερ ὑπέσταν.
    Χαῖρε Σελαναία λιπαρόχροε, χαίρετε κἆλλοι
    Ἀστέρες, εὐκάλοιο κατ' ἄντυγα Νυκτὸς ὀπαδοί.

Then fare-thee-well, dread Lady! turn thy coursers to the sea,
Be sure my task I will achieve, however hard it be;
Yes, fare-thee-well, thou Lady Moon! with face of shining light,
Farewell, ye other stars that grace the car of silent Night!

And Tibull. ii. 1, 87-90—

    Ludite: jam Nox jungit equos, currumque sequuntur
        Matris lascivo sidera fulva choro,
    Postque venit tacitus furvis circumdatus alis
        Somnus et incerto Somnia nigra pede.

    Sport on: Night yokes her steeds: with wanton tread
        The golden stars behind her chariot wheel;
    Then silent Sleep, with tawny wings outspread,
        And gloom-wrapt Dreams behind them tottering steal.

V. 172.   Vir tuus Tyrio in toro.

Cf. Tibull. i. 2, 73-76—

> Et te dum liceat teneris retinere lacertis,
> Mollis et inculta sit mihi somnus humo.
> Quid Tyrio recubare toro sine amore secundo,
> Prodest, cum fletu nox vigilanda venit?

> So while thy form my fond, fond arms retain,
> Be on the uncultured ground my slumbers light;
> Why press the Tyrian couch, if love disdain,
> And spend in tears the livelong weary night?

V. 211-225.

Cf. Stat. Silv. i. 2, 271-273—

> —— quumque tuos tacito Natura recessu
> Formarit vultus, multum de patre decoris,
> Plus de matre feras.

> When Nature, with mysterious hand, shall mould
> The tiny features of thine infant face,
> May we thy father's beauty there behold,
> And more than all thy mother's matchless grace.

Tibull. i. 7, 55, 56—

> At tibi succrescat proles, quae facta parentis
> Augeat et circa stet veneranda senem.

> And may a race be thine, to swell thy deeds,
> And stand in honour round their aged sire.

Mart. Epigr. vi. 27, 3, 4—

> Est tibi, quae patria signatur imagine vultus,
> Testis maternae nata pudicitiae.

>   To thee
> A child is born, the image of her sire,
> Sure witness of her mother's chastity.

And Theoc. Idyll. xvii. 43, 44—

 'Αστόργου δὲ γυναικὸς ἐπ' ἀλλοτρίῳ νόος αἰεί,
 'Ρηΐδιοι δὲ γοναί, τέκνα δ' οὐ ποτεοικότα πατρί.

But an unloving woman's thoughts aye round the stranger gather,
Her parturitions too are light—her sons unlike their father.

POEM LXII.

THIS nuptial song is probably an imitation of one of the lost hymenaeals of Sappho. The youths (*sponsi aequales*) are still reclining at the festal board of the bridegroom, when the rising of Vesper reminds them that the jubilant ceremonial is at hand. The bride meanwhile is being escorted home by a band of maidens (*virginis aequales*), who are now rapidly approaching the gates. After a few words from their respective leaders, calculated to excite feelings of emulation, the maidens fiercely denounce Vesper, while the youths as lustily proclaim his praises. The exceeding beauty and fitness of the relative parts of the poem are so apparent that remark on them by the translator would be superfluous.

CARM. LXII. v. 5.

 Hymen, O Hymenaee! Hymen ades O Hymenaee!

Cf. Theoc. Idyll. xviii. 59—

  Ὑμὴν ὦ Ὑμέναιε, γάμῳ ἐπὶ τῷδε χαρείης.

V. 7. Nimirum *Oetaeos ostendit noctifer ignes.*

Cf. Virg. Eclog. viii. 30—

  ——— tibi *deserit Hesperus Oetam.*

  For thee the star of eve leaves Oeta's hill.

V. 26. Hespere, qui coelo lucet jucundior ignis.

Cf. Hom. Il. xxii. 318—

"Εσπερος, ὃς κάλλιστος ἐν οὐρανῷ ἵσταται ἀστήρ.

Bion. xvi. 1—

"Εσπερε, τᾶς ἐρατᾶς χρύσεον φάος 'Αφρογενείας.

Virg. Aen. viii. 589-591—

Qualis, ubi oceani perfusus Lucifer unda,
Quem Venus ante alios astrorum diligit ignes,
Extulit os sacrum coelo, tenebrasque resolvit.

And Statii Silv. ii. 6, 36, 37—

——— quantum praecedit clara minores
Luna faces, quantumque alios premit Hesperus ignes.

V. 42. Multi illum pueri, multae optavere puellae.

Cf. Ovid. Met. iii. 353—

Multi illum juvenes, multae cupiere puellae.

V. 44. Nulli illum pueri, nullae optavere puellae.

Cf. Ovid. Met. iii. 355—

Nulli illum juvenes, nullae tetigere puellae.

Poem LXIII.

This poem—the grandest alike in conception and in execution of all the works of Catullus—is the only specimen of Galliambic poetry in the whole range of Latin literature.

Atys, the subject of the poem, is a beautiful youth, who, under the influence of a fearful frenzy, repairs with a chosen band of followers to the forests and mountain fastnesses of Phrygia, to celebrate the inhuman orgies of Cybele, the guardian goddess of the land.

From the opening lines, and from repeated passages throughout the poem, it may safely be inferred that this is not the celebrated Phrygian shepherd of the name so often mentioned by Greek and Roman mythologists, but most probably a Grecian youth of noble birth, who, carried away by an insane religious fervour, crossed to Phrygia to perform the awful rites practised by the votaries of the Queen of Dindymus. The subject and its treatment are in every sense original, and the Galliambic metre, being endless in its modifications, has afforded the poet ample scope for delineating the varied feelings and emotions of the unhappy youth. The frenzy of the votary; the raving madness of his Maenad crew; the dull languor of Atys consequent on his excitement; his withering despair on awaking to a sense of his degrading and hopeless servitude; his heart-rending wail on the recollection of his parents, his home, and the sports of his youth; the fierce ire of Cybele on learning the repentance of the recreant wretch, and his flight back to the dreary dens of Ida—are portrayed with a terrible power, that conjures up before our eyes the heart-rending spectacle in all the terrors of a living reality.

The accessories of time, place, and circumstance, moreover, are wondrously in keeping with the subject. Dancing and revelry occupy the dusky evening; darkness brings its balm to the wearied orgiast; the glories of sunrise awaken him to mock his misery; whilst the vast ocean below, the snow-capt Ida above, the stag bounding through the brushwood, and the boar rushing from the thicket, furnish the drapery for the scene of woe. In short, the originality, grandeur, and poetic spirit of the Atys, stamp Catullus as a genius of the highest order.

Few poets would have dared to strike the lyre for such a subject, fewer still could have risen to the requirements of the theme. Julius Scaliger, who had no liking for Catullus, was constrained to pronounce this poem *divine;* while Gibbon, in his " Decline and Fall," has spoken of it with unbounded admiration. Critics of our time do not scruple to tell us that it is *probably* a translation, but it were surely but bare justice to allow Catullus the authorship till something resembling it at least in subject and treatment is discovered in another language. We do not deny that he may have been to a certain extent indebted to his journey to the East for the groundwork of his poem, and that there he may have derived materials for its composition, but that, instead of being an argument against, is in our opinion the strongest one for, its originality. Be that as it may, it is a gorgeous memorial of a primeval worship. In its abrupt turns, broken cadences, and rattling pace, it is like the live thunder leaping from crag to crag over mountains wrapt in the impenetrable gloom of chaos and of night.

The final fate of the hapless wretch draws from Catullus the earnest prayer that he may never be the victim of such a frantic inspiration; while it has furnished Ovid with an appropriate curse in his fearful chapter of imprecations : *—

Mayst thou in Phrygian mode, like those whom awful Cybele incites,
Thy worthless members hack and hew, crazed votary of frantic rites,

* Ibis, 451-454.

Nor man nor woman be, but, Atys-like, a sexless wretch become,
And rattle with effeminate fingers on the hollow-sounding drum.

It would be futile to attempt to reproduce the Atys in an English dress in anything like its fire, impetuous roll, and gorgeous imagery. The highest aim of a translator can be little more than to give a tolerably accurate rendering of the *words*. Several Latin poems have been attempted in modern times in Galliambic measure, but all of them with indifferent success. Nor is this to be wondered at, when we consider the extraordinary merits of the only model. Perhaps the best known Galliambic poem of modern days is by Muretus, of which we subjoin a translation :—

BACCHUS.

My hair with ivy chaplets bound, I sing the father of the vine,
Lyaeus, Bromius, Evius, thigh-sprung, ever-young, whose power divine
Made vine-trees flourish, and new gifts shower'd on the world where'er they are—
New gifts to drive from weary hearts the carking cares of life afar.

O sire! O two-horn'd sire! for thee in mystic revel on we dash,
Thou slayer of the giant race, for thee the cymbals loud we clash,
For thee we wear dishevell'd hair, for thee we raise the jocund song,
For thee we toss our heads about, and the steep mountains course along.

The dreary forest haunts are moved, and echo back our hymns to thee,
Evöe! who givest sweet repose, and sett'st the troubled spirit free,

ILLUSTRATIVE NOTES. 243

Where'er thou dwellest lovely Venus has her flower-wreath'd temple there,
And tender Love, and Jest, and sprightly Mirth to swell thy train repair.

With fife and blare of horn the ambient air resounds, the dancers reel,
And baleful griefs and hateful cares afar with rapid footstep steal.
Ye ministers, here place the cups, and fill them to the brim with wine,
That I may slake my thirst and sate me with the purple juice divine.

'Twere sinful with dry lips to celebrate thy sacred mystic rites.
Vah! Vah! light-giving sire! what ardour now my burning heart excites!
A thousand strange undreamt-of lights burst on my heaven-illumined eyes,
Behold! behold! how now the grove all round with rapid whirlings flies.

See how the ground, beat in the wild careerings, starts and shakes,
And now the blare of horns upon my ears with sounds unwonted breaks.
Hence ye profane! the god! the god comes hurrying with his pliant lash in hand,
Guiding the dappled lynx and tiger fierce obedient to command.

Old rubicund Silenus, and the Satyrs' cloven-footed crew,
And troops of yelling Bacchants with impetuous steps the god pursue,
Evöe! great Bassareus! for ever to be feared, thrice, four times blest
Is he who plies thy rites, and shakes the ivied Thyrsus, scorning rest.

When thy fair mother, thunder-blasted, prematurely gave thee birth,
Jove bore thee in his thigh, lest incensed Juno should thee hurl to earth,
Then gave thee to be reared and cherished by the woodland-roaming sprites—
The nymphs who skip with nimble foot o'er Nysa's lofty mountain heights.

In childhood's days, where'er thy genial foot had trod, there round the trees
The circling vine its tender tendrils wound and flaunted in the breeze,
And where you play'd with youthful frolic, there the wine-fount 'gan to spring,
And smoothly flow'd the purple stream with low and gentle murmuring.

Why should I tell of Indian climes by thee to mild subjection brought?
The sinful deeds that Pentheus and Lycurgus in their madness wrought?
Or the strange monsters that appear'd within the blue Etruscan sea?
How could thy glories e'er be sung—thy trophies reckon'd up by me?

Tmolus, Cythaeron, Nisa felt thy power, and own'd thee as their lord;
Minstrels and poets celebrate thy majesty with one accord;
Whene'er thy nectar has been quaff'd the flame of genius fires the brain;
A-sudden all around resounds the music of the inspirèd strain.

Away from thee no joy, no sweet hilarity the soul can find,
Thou liftest care and sorrow's heavy burden from the weary mind,

All foolish shame thou dost efface, thou dost reveal the secret way;
Victorious o'er love's battle-plains thou rid'st—the darkness is thy day.

Then come, our father! come, our king! come, glory of the vaulted sky!
Oh, hither, hither come, and look on us with mild benignant eye.

Excursus V.

Galliambus.

The Galli are said to have received their name from the river Gallus in Phrygia—the cradle of the worship of Cybele. In their wild orgies they scoured the mountains and solitary places, goading themselves to frenzy with the lash (*Flagellum*), and accompanying their frantic song (*Galliambus*) with the music of cymbals, timbrels, and Phrygian flutes. The Galliambus, alike in structure and spirit, seems to be intimately connected with the ancient Grecian Dithyramb, the largest extant specimen of which is by Pindar, and has been preserved by Dionysius of Halicarnassus. Although Greece had many Dithyrambic poets, but few specimens of their songs have reached us, and the brevity of those which remain precludes the possibility of attaining anything like an accurate idea of the nature and structure of the verse. It was a wild and animated strain, and the buoyant spirit of the Greeks, and their musical and flexible language were peculiarly favourable to its development.

But the genius of the stern and severe Roman, and the unbending nature of his stately tongue must have proved antagonistic to its success, and it does not seem, notwithstanding Cicero's assertion to the contrary, ever to have been very popular with the poets of Rome. Horace has some noble lyrics—the very essence of impassioned poetry, and thoroughly Dithyrambic in spirit, but they are executed according to a regular system, and not in what we conceive to have been the mode of the Dithyramb, properly so called. One Latin Dithyrambic chorus, however, apparently genuine in spirit and treatment, is to be found in the Oedipus of Seneca. The Atys is, as we have said, the only extant specimen of Galliambic verse; and as it consists of only ninety-three lines, and these very variable in their structure, it is impossible to reduce it to any certain scheme of versification. Most probably it is to be referred to the same class as the Dithyramb of Pindar, of which Horace says:—

> . . . . Numerisque fertur
> Lege solutis,

and hence it were vain to try to reduce it to a system according to the canons of prosody. Like the Dithyramb, too, it was set in the Phrygian mode, and delighted in compound and anomalous epithets (*nova verba*). This latter feature is clearly exemplified in the Atys, as witness the compounds hederigerae, properipidem, sonipedibus, herifugae, sylvicultrix, &c.

CARM. LXIII. v. 5.

Devolsit ——— silice.

Cf. Ovid. Fast. iv. 233-244—

Hic furit, et credens thalami procumbere tectum
  Effugit, et cursu Dindyma summa petit.
Et modo "Tolle faces!" "Remove" modo "verbera"! clamat.
  Saepe Palaestinas jurat adesse deas.
Ille etiam saxo corpus laniavit acuto,
  Longaque in immundo pulvere tracta coma est.
Voxque fuit "Merui! meritas do sanguine poenas,
  A! pereant partes quae nocuere mihi!"
"A! pereant," dicebat adhuc, onus inguinis aufert
  Nullaque sunt subito signa relicta viri.
Venit in exemplum furor hic, mollesque ministri
  Caedunt jactatis vilia membra comis.

Then madness fastens on the youth—he thinks the roof will crash, and tremulous
Springs forth, and in his flight ascends the highest peaks of Dindymus.

And now "Remove the brands," he cries, and now "hence
  with the lash, begone!"
Often he swears the Furies at his heels are madly pressing on.
Then picks he up a pointed flint and maims his form with gashes
  vile,
And in the foul and miry dust his flowing tresses trail the while.
Aloud he cries, "With this my blood meet penalty I pay; 'tis
  right,
Perish the parts that wrought my sin,—perish they from my
  loathing sight."
"Ah! perish they!" again he cried, and then his sex away he
  shore,
And not a single trace remain'd to tell what Atys was before.
Hence, in all after-time, the mad effeminate crew, in wild despair,
Hack with the flints their members vile, and toss aloft their
  streaming hair.

V. 62, 63.

I have here followed the text of Schwabius—

> Quod enim genus figuraest ego non quod obierim?
> Ego mulier, ego adolescens, ego ephebus, ego puer.

V. 65, 66.

> Mihi januae frequentes, mihi limina tepida,
> Mihi floridis corollis redimita domus erat.

Cf. Lucret. iv. 1173-1175—

> At lacrimans exclusus amator limina saepe
> Floribus et sertis operit, postesque superbos,
> Ungit amaracino, et foribus miser oscula figit.

Propert. i. 16, 21, 22—

> Nullane finis erit nostro concessa dolori,
> Tristis et in tepido limine somnus erit?

Tibull. i. 2, 13, 14—

> Te meminisse decet, quae plurima voce peregi
> Supplice, cum posti florida serta darem.

> O think of all the vows that o'er and o'er
> I breathed with suppliant voice when all thy door
> I hung with flowery garlands.

And Theoc. Idyll. ii. 152—

> Καὶ φᾶτο οἱ στεφάνοισι τὰ δώματα τῆνα πυκάσδειν.

V. 92, 93.   Procul —— rabidos.

Cf. Tibull. i. 4, 67-70—

> At qui non audit Musas, qui vendit amorem,
>   Idaeae currus ille sequatur Opis,
> Et tercentenas erroribus expleat urbis,
>   Et secet ad Phrygios vilia membra modos.

> May those who scorn the Muse, and sell their love,
>   The chariot of Idaean Ops pursue,
> Careering, through three hundred cities rove,
>   And to the Phrygian notes their members hew.

Poem LXIV.

The "Peleus and Thetis" is a beautiful legendary poem, which Catullus has invested with all the charm and natural grace of Homeric song.

It partakes more of the nature of an Idyll or little Epos than of an Epithalamium, and if tried according to any other standard it will assuredly suffer, as unity or harmony in design seems to have been no part of the poet's purpose.

The episode of Ariadne occupies fully more than the

half of the poem, and, as it is into it that the poet has thrown his greatest strength, its effect exceeds that produced by the subject proper.

The poem opens with a brief allusion to the object of the Argonautic Expedition, and the building of the good ship Argo under the auspices of Athena. As soon as the virgin craft is bounding over the deep, the Nereids, astounded at the invasion of their hitherto undisputed dominion, start from their ocean-caves. The mortal is face to face with the immortal, and both are smitten with desire. Peleus is entranced with love for Thetis, and the daughter of the fair-haired Tethys does not spurn his hand. They are betrothed, the immortal parents of the fair immortal consenting to the union.

The poet, after duly invoking the heroes of the expedition, the ship in which they sailed on their perilous errand, and Peleus "the stay of Thessaly," details the preparations for the nuptials. The friends of Peleus, bearing with them rich offerings, hasten to Pharsalus to do honour to the illustrious pair. High and low hold jubilee, neglecting for the time their various concerns and avocations. The palace is adorned in a style of unequalled magnificence; gold and silver and ivory shine on wall and couch and board; but the great attraction is the gorgeous coverlet of the nuptial couch (*Lectus genialis*), on which is portrayed, among other things, with singular art and effect, the heroic legend of Theseus and Ariadne.

The poet, for a while, leaves his proper theme to relate the touching story as there told. This episode may be looked upon as his greatest effort, if we except the magnificent poem on Atys. From the moment that we are introduced to the anguish-wrung maiden on the barren shore of Naxos, till the appearance of

Bacchus and his crew, the interest never flags. Whether the poet leads us back to her hours of guileless girlhood, when, in the bosom of her family, she grows up like a myrtle on the banks of the Eurotas; or pictures her on the arrival of Theseus in Crete, smitten with love for the valorous youth, dowering him with life and glory, and confiding to him her young warm heart with all the ardour of trusting but misgiven devotion; or bids her denounce, in the acme of misery, the villain who had lured her from her home and left her to perish, the mind is enchained, the heart spontaneously sympathises, and the whole soul is thrilled with emotions that make us forget the poet and realise the scene. The skilful versifier may please the critical taste, his "callida junctura" may charm the ear, but it is the poet alone who can make us feel the joy or sorrow, the ecstasy or anguish of another.

Into this episode Catullus naturally introduces the parting of Aegeus and Theseus, and, though pathos is the chief characteristic of this part of the poem, we have no more pleasing instance of it than that evinced in the parting words of Aegeus to his son. By introducing this scene, and afterwards rendering due retribution to Theseus at the hand of Heaven, Catullus has shown us how far impartial recompense transcends partial reparation.

Ovid, in one of the passages appended below, has united Theseus in happy nuptials with Bacchus; Catullus, though he had an excellent opportunity, has refrained from so doing, and consequently, as Dunlop well observes, "he leaves the pity we feel for the abandonment of Ariadne unweakened on the mind." Still the blooming Bacchus and his crew, elsewhere portrayed on the embroidered coverlet, help to wean us from the hapless maiden. Catullus merely hints at the motive of

Bacchus, and immediately finds a congenial theme in describing the revelries and orgies of his votaries. We may remark that it is here that the poet most nearly approaches the spirit and wild grandeur of the Atys; in fact, it is only the difference in the measure that constitutes the difference in degree.

He is now prepared to return to the gay festivities of the spousals. But, ere the demigods and gods appear, it is meet that mortals should retire. Catullus in a few lines of transcendent beauty, in which he compares the withdrawal of the visitors to the retreating waves of ocean on the dawn of a summer morn, clears the palace, and the Centaur Chiron, the dweller on Pelion, who was one day to be the tutor of Achilles, comes with offerings of random-wreathed flowers from the hills and dales and river-banks of Thessaly.

Peneus next, a kinsman of the bride, and greatest of Thessalian river gods, comes with an appropriate gift of trees, wherewith to adorn the doors and vestibule of the palace.

Then enters rock-chained Prometheus, to whom Peleus was in great measure indebted for his bride. These demigods Catullus has chosen with great art and discernment, as each of them is in some respect connected either with the bride or bridegroom. After these comes Jupiter himself, attended by all the blessed immortals except Phoebus and Diana. The old poets of Greece tell us that all the deities were present except Atë, the goddess of discord, who was not invited. Catullus, with a clearer poetic insight and a nobler appreciation of the prescient character of Apollo, has excluded him from the number of the guests. The god of prophecy knew that he would slay their offspring, and Diana, as the goddess of chastity, would have been out of place ; but, apart from these considerations, Catullus expressly tells us that they hated Peleus.

The nuptial board is spread, the guests are seated; and the Parcae, while they spin the threads of fate, sing with shrill voices the destinies of the pair, and the prowess, achievements, and doom of their son. It is a splendid hymn, and its ever-recurrent refrain gives a wild and sombre effect to the prophetic canticle. Here, strictly speaking, ends the poem in so far as it concerns Peleus and Thetis. The poet, however, cannot conclude without contrasting the innocence and happiness of a brighter past with the guilt and misery of his own time. These concluding lines have a peculiar interest, for not only do they form a most appropriate epilogue, but they afford us the only instance of moral reflection in the works of our poet.

One word as to the claims of this poem to originality. Like the Atys, it is said by some to bear evidence of translation from the Greek. Hesiod, we know, wrote an Epithalamium in honour of Peleus and Thetis, but, as the poem of Catullus cannot be classed under that head, we may conclude that it is not an imitation or translation of it. Moreover, it is not in Hesiod's manner. Cicero, certainly, in one of his letters to Atticus, quotes a fragment from a Greek poet, of which the 111th line of this poem is a literal translation. It is possible that Catullus may have drawn extensively from that unknown author, but, considering the number of his lines that bear more or less resemblance to passages in many of the Greek poets, we will probably be nearer the truth if we conclude with Doering that Catullus has closely imitated no one writer, but rather, like Horace,

"apis Matinae
More modoque,"

has fluttered through the gardens of the Greeks, and extracted the choicest honey from their flowers.

Excursus VI.

ARIADNE AS TREATED BY OVID.

OVID has four times treated the subject of Ariadne—viz., in the "Art of Love," the "Heroides," the "Fasti," and the "Metamorphoses;" and in all of them he has in *expression* borrowed extensively from the episode in the "Peleus and Thetis." The first of these (A.A. i. 527-564) is undoubtedly a piece of very high merit, and is more than any of the others in the *manner* of Catullus. The barren shore of Naxos, the loneliness and anguish of Ariadne, her disordered person, her unutterable terror at the sudden appearance of Bacchus and his crew, the wild revelry of the Bacchanalians, and the seizure of the fainting maiden by the enamoured god, are depicted with great naturalness and effect. Here we have none of the quibbles and artificial points that are painfully apparent in two of the other pieces, and which, besides marring the general effect, are inconsistent with all ideas of

"Ariadne passioning
For Theseus' perjuries and unjust flight."

In such compositions we look not for point and finished sarcasm ; we only expect despair, reproach, and anguish—the vehement, spontaneous utterances of a breaking heart.

The Epistle (Her. x.) is unfortunately far too minute, and labours under the disadvantage of being read, as it were, secondhand.

The extract from the "Fasti," (lib. iii. 459-516,) which treats of the desertion of Ariadne by Bacchus, their reconciliation, and her apotheosis, has more energy than the last, but is overloaded with poetical conceits.

The passage from the "Metamorphoses" (lib. viii. 174-182,) consists of only a few lines, and is introduced by Ovid in his great poem for a specific purpose. It is quite free from the defects of the two pieces noticed immediately before ; and it is matter of regret that Ovid has not left us an Ariadne, *in extenso*, in the fine hexameters of which he was such a perfect master. Elegiac verse was hardly suited to a continued stretch of vehement passion and agonised denunciation. For comparison with the Ariadne of Catullus we subjoin the following translations :—

ARTIS AMAT., lib. i. 527–564.

Along the unknown sands the frantic Gnosian maiden roam'd,
Where wild by Dia's little isle the dashing billow foam'd ;
Loose-robed as when from sleep she rose, her heaving bosom bare,
Foot-naked, o'er her shoulders stream'd her golden-colour'd hair ;
She shouted, " Cruel Theseus," by the waves all deaf and cold,
While down her tender cheeks the bitter tears of anguish roll'd,
Shouted and wept at once ; yet both she did with seemly grace,
Nor did the tearful torrent mar the beauty of her face.
Now beating with her palms her breasts, that, ah ! too tender seem'd,
"The wretch has fled me ; what will now become of me?" she scream'd,
"What will become of me?" Along the shore the cymbals clash'd,
Loud boom'd the timbrel's airy round, with quivering fingers dash'd.
Froze on her tongue the half-lipp'd words ; with fear she swoon'd away;
No trace of blood remain'd within that form of hueless clay.
Lo ! there the Mimalonian dames scud with dishevell'd hair,
Lo ! the light-tripping Satyr crew before the god repair ;
Drunk old Silenus, on his crook-back'd ass, drives on the train ;
Scarce can he keep his seat, though holding firmly by the mane.
Now he pursued the Bacchants, now pursued they him, now fled ;
Anon with lash the unsteady rider plied his quadruped,
Till o'er the brute's long ears the swaggering creature headlong flies ;
The Satyrs shout around him : " Up ! O father ! up ! arise !"
Now in his grape-wreathed car the wine-god hurried on amain,
And to his harness'd tigers freely gave the golden rein.

Colour, memory, utterance, forsook the frenzy-stricken maid,
Thrice flight she sought, and thrice with fear her trembling feet
    were stay'd.
She shook, as shakes before the stormy wind the wheaten
    ear,
Or as the fragile reed that quivers in the marshy mere.
To whom the god: "Lo! here I come, a spouse more leal to
    thee,
"Fear not, O Gnosian girl, the wife of Bacchus thou shalt be;
Be heaven thy dower, in yonder sky thou'lt beam a radiant
    star,
"And oft the Cretan Crown will guide the doubtful mariner."
He spoke; and, lest the tigers should her timid heart affright,
Leap'd from his chariot, dashed across the sand with footstep
    light,
And clasp'd her to his bosom, powerless to resist his nod,
Then bore her off—how easy all, if willing be the god.
Some "Hymen" sing, some "Evöe" shout, caressing and
    carest,
Soon lie the maiden and the god in holy nuptials blest.

OVID. Her. x. (45–64.)

45 What could I do but let mine eyes outpour the bitter tear,
    When o'er the boundless waste they saw thy canvas dis-
        appear?
    Now o'er the wilderness I wandered with dishevell'd hair,
    Like Bacchant by the wine-god roused to frenzied, dark
        despair;
    Now, gazing forward on the sea, sat frozen on the stone;
50 My seat a stone—a stone myself—I motionless made moan;
    And then I sought the couch again on which we both re-
        clined,
    It could not render back its trust—no—thee I could not
        find.
    I touch'd the prints thy feet had made—'twas all I could
        for thee;
    I touch'd the bed thy limbs had warm'd, when thou wast
        there with me.

55 I laid me down—my flowing tears stream'd on the couch
   like rain;
   We both have press'd thee, I exclaimed, give back, give
   back the twain!
   A pair we here together came—why not depart a pair?
   Perfidious couch! where is the greater part of me, oh where?
   What shall I do? where shall I go forlorn? oh wretched
   fate!
60 No trace of man or beast is here, the isle is desolate;
   Its every shore sea-girdled round. A sailor? there is none.
   A ship to brave the dangerous ways? Alas! there is not
   one!
   Grant that I had companions, winds, a ship at my com-
   mand :
   What then? my kindred would debar me from my native
   land.

(99–132.)

99 Would that Androgeos still had lived! nor thou, Cecropian land,
   Hadst e'er atoned for his foul fate with victims from thy
   strand,
   Nor, Theseus, that thy strong right arm, with club of
   gnarlèd oak,
   Had dealt against the Minotaur the murder-freighted stroke;
   Nor that my hands had brought the thread—a gift thou
   didst not spurn—
   And placed within thy reach what means ensured thy safe
   return.
105 Yet surely I should marvel not that victory crown'd thy
   toil,
   And that the prostrate monster stain'd with gore the Cretan soil;
   For never could his horns transfix a heart of hardest steel,
   No, though thou hadst no corselet, all secure thou still
   mightst feel,
   For in thy breast thou hadst nor flint nor adamant alone,
110 But thou hadst Theseus too, and he is harder far than
   stone.

O cruel sleep! why held'st thou seal'd my weary orbs of sight?
Yet would that I had then been whelm'd in everlasting night!
O cruel winds! too favouring thus to let the villain go,
And gales! officious but to plunge my soul in deepest woe.
115 O cruel right hand! that my brother slew and murder'd me,
And troth pledged at my loving quest, a name! a mockery!
Sleep, winds, and troth have all conspired against a hapless maid,
And by a triple treason thus I singly am betray'd.

And shall I die, nor see a mother's tears of pity more?
120 Shall no kind fingers close mine eyes when life's last struggle's o'er?
Breathed on a foreign air shall my sad spirit leave my breast?
Nor friendly hands anoint my limbs for ever laid at rest?
And shall my bones be pick'd by ravenous birds that scour the sea?
Is such a grave meet recompense for all I've done for thee?

125 Thou'lt seek Cecropia's ports; and, welcomed to thy native land,
When, glory-crown'd, before thy wondering, gape-mouth'd crowd thou'lt stand,
And proudly tell how thou the savage Minotaur didst slay,
And paint his rocky dwelling cut with many a dubious way,
Tell, too, thou'st left a luckless girl on this lone strand to pine;
130 That deed should form some title to the fame that will be thine.
Aegeus was not thy father, Aethra ne'er gave birth to thee;
132 The authors of thy being were the rocks and ruthless sea.

R

OVID. FAST. (459–516.)

459 On the succeeding night the Gnosian crown thou wilt descry.
Through Theseus' cruel wrong the Gnosian maiden reach'd the sky;
She, who had saved her thankless spouse with clew of slender thread,
Had now well changed her perjured lord's for youthful Bacchus' bed.
Proud of her lot, why did I weep, poor rustic girl? she said,
His very perfidy has shower'd rare honours on my head.

465 Meanwhile the tribes of Ind the hair-trimm'd god could not withstand,
And, booty-laden, home he comes from that far eastern land,
And 'mong the maids of radiant form—the rosy victor's prize—
One girl, the daughter of their king, found favour in his eyes.
Then wept his loving wife, and, roaming o'er the curvèd shore
470 With streaming hair, such words as these did Ariadne pour:

"Ye waves! again to like complaints, oh lend your listening ears!
Lo! once again, ye sands! I pray, receive my bitter tears.
Once cried I—words remember'd well—'false Theseus and accurst;'
He left me—now my second lord is treacherous as the first.
475 'Henceforth let woman ne'er trust man,' again I will exclaim;
The name of my deceiver's changed—my story is the same.
Oh! would I had fulfill'd the fate that threaten'd me before!
My bitter tears had all been wept, and I had been no more.

Why didst thou save me? Bacchus! why? on yon bleak
    desert cast,
480 I could have drain'd my cup at once, and all had now been
    past.

" Oh! more unstable than the leaves that round thy
    temples twine,
Unstable Bacchus! thou hast known what anguish once
    was mine,
And hast thou dared to bring a foreign quean to pain my
    sight,
And rob our bridal bower of bliss, our chamber of de-
    light?
485 Alas! where is thy troth? and where the oaths thou once
    didst swear?
Ah, me! how often shall I breathe those words of drear
    despair?
Theseus thou blam'dst, thou call'dst him base, a maiden to
    undo ;
Be judge thyself, thou 'lt say thou art the baser of the two.

" Silence brood o'er my wrong! let silent griefs my soul
    consume,
490 Lest haply I, so oft deceived, seem worthy of my doom.
But least of all let Theseus know—thou surely never wilt—
He would rejoice that thou hadst been partaker of his
    guilt.

" Forsooth, a girl of fairer hue supplants thy swarthy queen,
Then be it so, and in my foe be that hue ever seen,
495 What matters it? that fault with thee's the rarest of her
    charms ;
What art thou doing? thou but clasp'st pollution in thine
    arms.
Bacchus! fulfil thy pledge—prefer no other's love to mine,
For all that wife could ever give, all, husband, has been
    thine.

"The horns of a too beauteous bull once won my mother's heart,
500 Thine, Ariadne's: mine the sad, but hers the shameless part.
Let not my love turn to my hurt, for it hath hurt not thee
That thou confessedst all the flame thy bosom felt for me;
Nor think it strange thou burn'dst me—thou, 'tis said, in fire wast born,
And by thy father's hand from its devouring fury torn.
505 And am I she whom thou of yore didst vow to dower with heaven?
Ah me! what was thy promise then! and what return thou 'st given!"

She finished. Long her woeful plaint fell on her husband's ear,
For haply he had follow'd close on Ariadne's rear;
He clasps her in one long embrace, kisses her tears away,
510 And says, "Let us together seek the realms of endless day;
My wife before—now from my name united name thou 'lt draw,
Be Ariadne now no more, but henceforth Libera;
And of thy godhead let thy crown a sure memorial be—
The crown which Vulcan Venus gave, which Venus gave to thee."
515 His word 's fulfill'd; its nine bright gems to nine bright stars he turns,
And 'mong the stellar hosts her crown with radiant splendour burns.

METAMM. viii. 174-182.

Then Theseus off to Dia's isle fair Ariadne bore,
And, cruel, left her there to roam the bleak and barren shore;
But when Iacchus saw the maid forlorn and sore distrest,
He brought her sweet deliverance, and clasp'd her to his breast,
And that to her a fadeless wreath of glory might be given,
He took the crown from off her brow and bore it up to heaven;

ILLUSTRATIVE NOTES. 261

Through unsubstantial fields of air it soar'd, and, soaring, burn'd
Till all its splendour-darting gems to lustrous stars were turn'd,
Then, 'tween the Serpent-holder and the Toiler-kneeling-down,
He hung it, still retaining all the semblance of a crown.

CARM. LXIV. v. 6, 7.

Ausi ——— palmis.

Cf. Tibull. i. 3, 35-38—

Quam bene Saturno vivebant rege prius quam
Tellus in longas est patefacta vias!
Nondum caeruleas pinus contempserat undas,
Effusum ventis praebueratque sinum.

How blest men lived when good old Saturn reign'd,
Ere roads had intersected hill and dale,
No pine had yet the azure wave disdain'd,
Or spread its swelling canvas to the gale.

V. 8, 9.   Diva ——— currum.

Cf. Aesch. Prom. Vinct. 467, 468—

Θαλασσόπλαγκτα δ' οὔτις ἄλλος ἀντ' ἐμοῦ
Λινόπτερ' ηὗρε ναυτίλων ὀχήματα.

And Shelley, Prom. Unbound, act ii. scene 4—

He taught to rule, as life directs the limbs,
The tempest-wingèd chariots of the ocean,
And the Celt knew the Indian.

V. 15. Aequoreae monstrum Nereides admirantes.

Cf. the picture of Boreas scouring the sea from the Cynegetica of Nemesianus, a Carthaginian poet (fl. 283 A.D.) v. 272-278—

Haud secus effusis Nerei per caerula ventis,
Quum se Threicius Boreas super extulit antro,
Stridentique sono vastas exterruit undas,
Omnia turbato cesserunt flamina ponto;

Ipse super fluctus spumanti murmure fervens,
Conspicuum pelago caput eminet; omnis euntem
Nereidum mirata suo super aequore turba.

As, when the unbridled winds o'er ocean rave,
Wild Boreas rushes from his Thracian cave,
And shrilly-roaring ploughs the immeasured plain,
Scaring his brothers from the writhing main
'Mid seething murmurs and with frantic glee,
He rears his head above the angry sea,
And onward sweeps. the liquid realms along,
Beheld with wonder by the Nereid throng.

V. 30.

Oceanusque, mari totum qui amplectitur or

Cf. Aesch. Prom. Vinct. 137-140—

Τῆς πολυτέκνου Τηθύος ἔκγονα
Τοῦ περὶ πᾶσάν θ' ἑλισσομένου
Χθόν' ἀκοιμήτῳ ῥεύματι παῖδες
Πατρὸς Ὠκεανοῦ.

V. 31, *seqq.*

Cf. Statii Theb. ii. 213-216—

. . . . Diffuderat Argos
Expectata dies: laeto regalia coetu
Atria complentur, species est cernere avorum
Cominus, et vivis certantia vultibus aera.

O'er Argos rose the day expected long,
And joyous crowds the regal palace throng,
Whose spacious halls ancestral figures grace,
The brazen vying with the living face.

V. 38, *seqq.*

Cf. Tibull. ii. 1, 5-8—

Luce sacra requiescat humus, requiescat arator,
Et grave suspenso vomere cesset opus.
Solvite vincla jugis: nunc ad praesepia debent
Plena coronato stare boves capite.

ILLUSTRATIVE NOTES. 263

    Let soil and tiller keep this feast alway,
      Suspend the share; be no hard labour here;
    Unchain the yokes; at well-fill'd stalls to-day
      'Tis meet with garlands ye should crown the steer.

V. 48, 49.

Cf. Hor. Sat. ii. 6, 102—

    In locuplete domo vestigia; rubro ubi cocco
    Tincta super lectos canderet vestis eburnos.

V. 52.

    Namque fluentisono prospectans littore Diae.

Dia, one of the Cyclades, afterwards called Naxos.

Theocritus thus alludes to the desertion of Ariadne by Theseus. Idyll. ii. 43-46—

    'Ες τρὶς ἀποσπένδω καὶ τρὶς τάδε πότνια φωνῶ·
    Εἴτε γυνὰ τήνῳ παρακέκλιται εἴτε καὶ ἀνήρ,
    Τόσσον ἔχοι λάθας, ὅσσόν ποκα Θησέα φαντί
    'Εν Δίᾳ λασθῆμεν ἐϋπλοκάμω 'Αριάδνας.

Dread queen, I thrice libation pay and thrice these words declare,
Or man or woman hath his heart entrapp'd in silken snare,
The oblivion seize him which they say from Theseus' breast erewhile
Swept fair-hair'd Ariadne left on Dia's lonely isle.

V. 90.

    Aurave distinctos educit verna colores.

Cf. Burns—

    Her looks were like a flower in May,
    Her smile was like a summer morn.

V. 96.

    Quaeque regis Golgos, quaeque Idalium frondosum.

Cf. Theoc. Idyll. xv. 100—

    Δέσποιν', ἃ Γολγώς τε καὶ 'Ιδάλιον ἐφίλησας.

V. 98.
———in flavo saepe hospite suspirantem !

Cf. Ovid. Fast. i. 417—
Hanc cupit, hanc optat, sola suspirat in illa.

V. 105–109.
Nam———frangens.

Cf. Virg. Aeneid. ii. 626–631—
Ac veluti summis antiquam in montibus ornum
Quum ferro accisam crebrisque bipennibus instant
Eruere agricolae certatim ; illa usque minatur,
Et tremefacta comam concusso vertice nutat,
Vulneribus donec paulatim evicta supremum
Congemuit, traxitque jugis avulsa ruinam.

As when on mountain top the aged ash,
Lopp'd by the steel and axe's frequent stroke,
Begins to totter 'neath repeated blows,
Then nods with threatening mien its palsied head
And shakes its quivering locks, till by degrees
With many wounds o'ercome it groans its last,
And, wrench'd away, drags ruin o'er the ridge.

Cf. also Hor. Od. iv. 6, 9–11—
—— mordaci velut icta ferro
Pinus, aut impulsa. cupressus Euro
Procidit late.

V. 111.
Nequidquam vanis jactantem cornua ventis.

Evidently taken from a Greek poet quoted by Cicero. Epist. ad Atticum, viii. 5—

——————— ῥίψαι
Πολλὰ μάτην κερδέσσιν ἐς ἠέρα θυμήναντα.

V. 132, *seqq.*
Tibullus alludes to the complaint of Ariadne, iii. 6, 39–42—
Gnosia, Theseae quondam perjuria linguae
Flevisti ignoto sola relicta mari :

Sic cecinit pro te doctus, Minoi, Catullus
Ingrati referens impia facta viri.

Fair Gnosian, erst the lies of Theseus' tongue
  Thou mourn'dst, left lone beside an unknown sea,
In thy behalf thus skill'd Catullus sung,
  And told the ingrate's fell impiety.

V. 140, 141.

——mihi non hoc miserae sperare jubebas :
Sed connubia laeta, sed optatos hymenaeos :

Cf. Claudian Rapt. Proserp. lib. iii.—

Non tales gestare tibi, Proserpina, taedas
Sperabam ; sed vota mihi communia matrum,
Et thalami festaeque faces, coeloque canendus
Ante oculos Hymenaeus erat : sic numina fatis
Volvimur, et nullo Lachesis discrimine saevit ?

My daughter, torch like this for thee I never hoped to bear,
And yet my wish was but the wish of mothers everywhere,
A happy bridal for my child, glad flambeaux flaming high,
A joyous hymenaeal sung beneath the open sky,
Thus 'mong the gods shall Lachesis without distinction rave,
And the dread name of deity be impotent to save?

V. 141.

Virgil has imitated this line, Aeneid. iv. 316—

Per connubia nostra, per inceptos hymenaeos.

V. 142.

Quae cuncta aerii discerpunt irrita venti.

Cf. Virg. Aeneid. ix. 312, 313—

——————————— sed aurae
Omnia discerpunt et nubibus irrita donant.

V. 154, *seqq.* Quaenam te genuit, &c.

Cf. Tibull. iii. 4, 83-96 —

Nec tibi crediderim votis contraria vota
Nec tantum crimen pectore inesse tuo :

> Nam te nec vasti genuerunt aequora ponti,
>   Nec flammam volvens ore Chimaera fero,
> Nec canis anguinea redimitus terga caterva,
>   Cui tres sunt linguae, tergeminumque caput,
> Scyllaque virgineam canibus succincta figuram,
>   Nec te conceptam saeva leaena tulit,
> Barbara nec Scythiae tellus horrendave Syrtis,
>   Sed culta et duris non habitanda domus.
> Et longe ante alias omnes mitissima mater
>   Isque pater quo non alter amabilior.
> Haec deus in melius crudelia somnia vertat
>   Et jubeat tepidos irrita ferre Notos.

Oh, I could ne'er believe thy vows were contrary to mine,
Or that so fell a thought could dwell within that heart of thine,
For roaring sea ne'er gender'd thee, nor from her jaws of fire
Did dread Chimaera belch thee forth—the offspring of her ire,
Nor wild hell-hound enwreath'd around with wriggling snakes
  thee bred,
Grim monster of the triple tongue and triple-formèd head,
Nor yet did maiden Scylla's dog-encinctured form thee bear,
Nor savage lioness conceive and whelp thee in her lair,
Nor was the barbarous Scythian land thy home or Syrtis fell,
But a benignant hearth where cruel beings could not dwell;
A mild fond mother, too, was thine, yea mild beyond compare,
No kindlier father ever nursed his child with kindlier care.
Then, gracious Heaven, conduct my cruel dreams to issues
  bright,
And bid warm Notus sweep these dark forebodings from my
  sight.

V. 171, 172.

> Jupiter omnipotens, utinam ne tempore primo
> Gnosia Cecropiae tetigissent littora puppes.

Cf. Virg. Aeneid. iv. 657, 658—

> Felix, heu nimium felix, si littora tantum
> Nunquam Dardaniae tetigissent nostra carinae!

Happy, alas! too happy had we been
If never Trojan keel had touch'd our strand!

V. 177.   Nam quo me referam?

Cf. Eurip. Med. 502, 503, &c.—

Νῦν ποῖ τράπωμαι; πότερα πρὸς πατρὸς δόμους,
Οὕς σοι προδοῦσα καὶ πάτραν ἀφικόμην; κ. τ. λ.

Where shall I turn me? To my father's halls?
I, who betray'd my home and fatherland
And came with thee? &c.

V. 192-194.   Quare —— iras.

Cf. Senec. Med. act i. v. 13, 14—

Adeste, adeste! Sceleris ultrices deae,
Crinem solutis squalidae serpentibus.

V. 205, 206.

Quo tunc et tellus atque horrida contremuerunt
Aequora, concussitque micantia sidera mundus..

Cf. Hor. Od. i. 34, 9-12—

Quo bruta tellus, et vaga flumina,
Quo Styx et invisi horrida Taenari
Sedes, Atlanteusque finis
Concutitur.

Whereat the inert earth with terror quakes,
Tremble the streams and rolling Stygian river,
The rocky cliff of hated Taenarus shakes,
And all the peaks of mighty Atlas quiver.

V. 247-249.   Sic —— recepit.

Cf. Stat. Silv. iii. 3, 179, 180—

———Haud aliter gemuit perjuria Theseus,
Littore quo falsis deceperat Aegea velis.

V. 260.
> Pars obscura cavis celebrabant orgia cistis.

Cf. Theocr. Idyll. xxvi. 7–9—
> Ἱερὰ δ'ἐκ κίστας πεποναμένα χερσὶν ἑλοῖσαι
> Εὐφάμως κατέθεντο νεοδρέπτων ἐπὶ βωμῶν,
> Ὡς ἐδίδασχ', ὡς αὐτὸς ἐθυμάρει Διόνυσος.

V. 270, *seqq*.

Cf. Shelley, Queen Mab, viii. 23, 24—
> Like the vague sighings of the wind at even
> That wakes the wavelets of the slumbering sea.

V. 274.
> ———leni resonant plangore cachinni.

Cf. Aesch. Prom. Vinct. 89, 90—
> ————————ποντίων τε κυμάτων
> Ἀνήριθμον γέλασμα.

Milton—
> Cheer'd with the grateful smell, old ocean *smiles*.

And Byron, "Giaour"—
> There mildly *dimpling*, ocean's cheek
> Reflects the tints of many a peak,
> Caught by the *laughing* tides that lave
> Those Edens of the eastern wave.

See also the beautiful lines of Martial, descriptive of the sea in a state of active repose. Epigr. x. 11–15—
> Hic summa leni stringitur Thetis vento;
> Nec languet aequor; viva sed quies Ponti
> Pictam phaselon adjuvante fert aura;
> Sicut puellae non amantis aestatem
> Mota salubre purpura venit frigus.

> Soft as from waving fan of lady fair
> Comes the cool breath that soothes the sultry air,
> So here the light wind plays on Thetis' breast,
> Who lies all still, yet not by languors prest;

Her living rest, and the light favouring breeze
The painted pinnace carry o'er the seas.

V. 278.

Ad se quisque vago passim pede discedebant.

Cf. Hom. Il. i. 606—

Οἱ μὲν κακκείοντες ἔβαν οἰκόνδε ἕκαστος.

V. 297, 298.

Quam quondam silici restrictus membra catena
Persolvit, pendens e verticibus praeruptis.

Cf. Aesch. Prom. Vinct. 4-6—

————————τόνδε πρὸς πέτραις
Ὑψηλοκρήμνοις τὸν λεωργὸν ὀχμάσαι
Ἀδαμαντίνων δεσμῶν ἐν ἀρρήκτοις πέδαις.

V. 306, 307.

The Parcae, who dwelt in the clefts of Parnassus (Hom. Hymn in Mercur. 555), and in the vicinity of Thessaly, are most fitly chosen by Catullus to sing the nuptial song. They sang the hymenaeus in honour of the nuptials of Jupiter and Juno, as we learn from the "Birds" of Aristophanes, *v.* 1731, *seqq.*—

> Back, divide, retire aside,
>   Away, 'tis now your duty
> Round the happy man to veer,
> Happy fortune's happiest peer,
>   Oh what loveliness is here,
>   And oh, what matchless beauty.
>
> Hail, blest bridegroom, who hast brought
>   Great joy to this our city,
> Great good luck by thee, I ween,
> Shower'd upon the birds has been;
>   Up, receive him and his queen
>   With bridal song and ditty.

Once upon a time the Fates
   With all the gods together
Did the lofty-thronèd king
To Olympian Juno bring,
And this hymenaeal sing,
   "Haste, Hymen, Hymen, hither."

Eros of the golden wing,
   And bloom no blast can wither,
Seized the back-stretch'd reins and drove,
Groomsman at the feast of love,
When blest Juno pair'd with Jove,
   "Haste, Hymen, Hymen, hither."

V. 331, 332.

Quae tibi flexanimo mentem perfundat amore,
Languidulosque paret tecum conjungere somnos.

Cf. Theoc. Idyll. xviii. 55, 56—

Εὕδετ' ἐς ἀλλάλων στέρνον φιλότατα πνέοντες
Καὶ πόθον.

Now sleep, and breathe into each other's breasts the fire
Of warm marital love and ever-fond desire.

V. 350–352.   Saepe ——— palmis.

Cf. Senec. Herc. Oet. 1668–1673—

Ingemuit omnis turba, nec lacrimas dolor
Cuiquam remisit. Mater in luctum furens
Diduxit avidum pectus, atque utero tenus
Exerta vastos ubera in planctus ferit;
Superosque et ipsum vocibus pulsans Jovem
Implevit omnem voce feminea locum.

Wail'd all the crowd; no tearless eye was there;
Then, wild with woe and frantic with despair,
His sorrowing mother bared her eager breast,
And smote with mighty blows her heaving chest,
While, blaming Jove and all the powers on high,
With wailings wild she fill'd the earth and sky.

V. 398 to the end.
>   Sed ——— claro.

Cf. Ovid. Metamm. i. 144-150—
>   ——— non hospes ab hospite tutus,
> Non socer a genero; fratrum quoque gratia rara est.
> Imminet exitio vir conjugis, illa mariti :
> Lurida terribiles miscent aconita novercae :
> Filius ante diem patrios inquirit in annos.
> Victa jacet pietas, et virgo caede madentes,
> Ultima Caelestum, terras Astraea reliquit.

> No guest of hospitable roof is sure ;
> No more is sire from son-in-law secure ;
> Even brothers' love has all or well-nigh fled ;
> The wife and husband wish each other dead ;
> Dire step-dames mix the lurid aconite ;
> The son abhors his very father's sight,
> And pries into his years with anxious care ;
> Affection prostrate lies.
>   Then Justice fair,
> The last lone lingerer of heavenly birth,
> Aghast with horror, fled the blood-soak'd earth.

POEM LXV.

CATULLUS had promised to translate for his friend Hortalus (Quintus Hortensius) the "Hair of Beronice," from Callimachus, a task which the death of his brother prevented him for a time from accomplishing. Afraid lest Hortalus should assign a false reason for the delay, or deem him guilty of forgetfulness, he lays bare his heart to his friend, and tells him his affliction with an openness of which only generous natures are capable.

In regard to the simile with which the poem concludes, the translator, while acknowledging its beauty, is compelled to side with those who fail to see its appositeness. He is inclined to think with Rossbach that it is either a fragment of a translation from Callimachus, or, at all events, a fragment of another poem. As the lines, however, are printed in almost every edition as the conclusion of the piece, he has given them the only rendering of which, considered as belonging to the poem, they seemed susceptible.

CARM. LXV. v. 1.

> Etsi me assiduo confectum cura dolore.

Cf. the opening lines of the Ciris —

> Etsi me vario jactatum laudis amore
> Irritaque expertum fallacis praemia volgi.

V. 13, 14.

> Qualia sub densis ramorum concinit umbris
> Daulias, absumti fata gemens Ityli.

Cf. Ovid. Heroid. xv. 153-156 —

> Sola virum non ulta pie maestissima mater
> Concinit Ismarium Daulias ales Ityn.
> Ales Ityn, Sappho desertos cantat amores
> Hactenus, ut media caetera nocte silent.

> Dire vengeance his lone mother brings
>   Upon her lord in mortal hate,
> And now, a Daulian bird, she sings
>   And mourns Ismarian Itys' fate.
> A bird o'er Itys lost complains,
>   And love-lorn Sappho sadly pours
> O'er slighted loves her rueful strains,
>   When all is still at midnight hours.

V. 19, 20.

> Ut missum sponsi furtivo munere malum
> Procurrit casto virginis e gremio.

Cf. Propert. i. 3, 21-33—

> Et modo solvebam nostra de fronte corollas
>   Ponebamque tuis, Cynthia, temporibus,
> Et modo gaudebam lapsos formare capillos,
>   Nunc furtiva cavis poma dabam manibus,
> Omniaque ingrato largibar munera somno,
>   Munera de prono saepe voluta sinu ;
> Et quotiens raro duxti suspiria motu,
>   Obstupui vano credulus auspicio,
> Ne qua tibi insolitos portarent visa timores,
>   Neve quis invitam cogeret esse suam :
> Donec diversas percurrens luna fenestras,
>   Luna moraturis sedula luminibus,
> Compositos levibus radiis patefecit ocellos.

And now I loosed the garland from my brow,
  And round thy temples did a chaplet twine,
Anon thy truant locks confined, and now
  My hand the furtive apple slipp'd in thine.

Ungrateful sleep with all my gifts I dower'd,
  Gifts that too oft have roll'd from forth thy breast,
And when thou stirr'dst or heav'dst a sigh, o'erpower'd
  I silent stood by bodings vain opprest,

Lest grim unwonted fears disturb'd thy dreams,
  Or eager swain, with thee unwilling, coped,
Then mild-ray'd Luna with officious beams
  Stream'd through the lattice, and thine eyelids oped.

Poem LXVI.

Beronice's Hair.

This poem is translated from the Greek of Callimachus —the poet whom, after Sappho, Catullus most delighted to reproduce. The following are the circumstances which induced the Greek poet to write this complimentary elegiac poëm.

Ptolemy Philadelphus, son of Ptolemy Soter (*the Preserver*), had caused a temple to be erected to his wife, Arsinöe, to whom he wished that divine honours should be paid. His son, Ptolemy Euergetes (*the Benefactor*), married his cousin-german, Beronice, daughter of Magas, king of Cyrene. In virtue of this relationship by blood, Beronice, in the poem, is styled, according to ancient usage, the sister of Ptolemy, (v. 17.) Very shortly after their union, the youthful husband was summoned from her side to fight the Assyrian. Beronice, in an agony of despair at the double loss of husband and brother, vows to devote a lock of her hair to the Gods if her husband should prove victorious and soon return to her arms in triumph. He returns, and the ruthless steel dissevers the lock from the head of the youthful queen. It is laid on the shrine of Arsinöe, and shortly after disappears. Light-winged Zephyr, brother of Memnon (*Unigena*, v. 53) and son of Aurora (Hes. Theog. v. 378), is commissioned by Venus to hasten to the temple and bear to heaven this tribute of conjugal devotion. He takes it up, and deposits it on the bosom of the Queen of Love, by whose command it is placed in the sky—

"A new-made star amid the primal spheres."

But the lock cannot forget the radiant brow of Beronice,

or the golden curls among which it used to play. It implores young brides to propitiate heaven in its behalf with offerings of perfumes, and declares that it would rather again adorn the brow of Beronice, than remain among the splendid throng, though chaos should ensue and all the stars be hurled from their places.

Such is a brief outline of the poem. The explanation of the mysterious disappearance of the lock, and its subsequent apotheosis, were invented by the shrewd and ingenious court-astronomer, Conon, to console the afflicted Beronice. Callimachus saw the value of the philosopher's pretended discovery, and embalmed it in the beautifully extravagant lines of which only an echo remains to us in the translation by Catullus. The heroism, tenderness, and devotion of Beronice are so well portrayed by the sorrowing lock that the poet, even without anything else to recommend him, must, by this work, have secured the favour and gratitude of the Egyptian queen.

Although we have every reason to believe that the translation was admirably executed by Catullus, the loss of the original is much to be regretted. No work of Catullus has suffered more from the inaccuracies and carelessness of transcribers, and the unhappy conjectural emendations of commentators, than this one; and the original would not only have afforded the means of restoring it to a certain extent, but would have exhibited to us, in a clearer light than we can ever possess, the extraordinary ability of Catullus in rendering the productions of the Greek poets. That he possessed this power in no ordinary degree will be at once apparent to any one who will take the trouble of comparing the structure of the elegiac poems of Catullus with that of the Greek elegies. The simplicity (ἀφέλεια), or Greek *abandon*, so to speak, of the Catullian distich is most marked when it is viewed side by side with the more exact and laboured productions of Ovid, Tibullus, and Propertius,—a characteristic not confined to his longer poems, but pervading all his epigrams.

CARM. LXVI. v. 1-6.
   Omnia —— aërio.
Cf. Aesch. Prom. Vinct. 457, 458—
   ———— ἔς τε δή σφιν ἀντολὰς ἐγὼ
   Ἄστρων ἔδειξα τάς τε δυσκρίτους δύσεις.

And Shelley, Prom. Unbound, Act ii., Scene 4—
 He taught the implicated orbits woven
 Of the wide-wandering stars; and how the sun
 Changes his lair, and by what secret spell
 The pale moon is transform'd, when her broad eye
 Gazes not on the inter-lunar sea.

V. 13.
  Dulcia nocturnae portans vestigia rixae.
Cf. Claudian. in Fescenn. Epith. Hon. et Mar—
  Nocturni referens vulnera proelii.

V. 48-50. Jupiter —— duritiem!
Cf. Aesch. Prom. Vinct. 500-503—
  ————ἔνερθε δὲ χθονὸς
  Κεκρυμμέν᾽ ἀνθρώποισιν ὠφελήματα
  Χαλκὸν, σίδηρον, ἄργυρον, χρυσόν τε τίς
  Φήσειεν ἂν πάροιθεν ἐξευρεῖν ἐμοῦ;

Cf. also v. 714, 715—
  Λαιᾶς δὲ χειρὸς οἱ σιδηροτέκτονες
  Οἰκοῦσι Χάλυβες, οὓς φυλάξασθαί σε χρή.

V. 91.
  Unguinis expertem non siris esse tuam me.

This is the reading given in the latest German editions, *e.g.* those of Rossbach, Schwabe, &c. Mr Ellis, in his edition of Catullus lately published, has retained the MS. reading *sanguinis*, which gains considerable support from the following passage in the "History" of Tacitus, (ii. 3):—"Sanguinem arae obfundere vetitum : precibus et igne puro altaria adolentur." The following is submitted as a rendering of the passage (v. 89 to the end), according to the text of Mr Ellis :—

> And when, O queen, thou to the stars shalt turn,
> And festal torches to Love's goddess burn,
> Forget me not before her bloodless shrine,
> For I, though here, am still as surely thine.
> Rush, stars, to ruin in your shady sky,
> Might I again amid her tresses lie!
> Let me but grace again thy brow divine,
> Orion then may next Aquarius shine.

Poems LXVIII.[a] and LXVIII.[b]

I HAVE followed Froelich and Rossbach in dividing this poem,—the first (v. 1-40) being addressed to Manlius; the second (v. 41-160) to Allius. The grounds for addressing the second to Allius are very questionable;* but there can be no doubt that the one poem has no relation to the other, and for the following reasons :—

1*st*. It is evident that Manlius had requested Catullus to send him some books, and to write him a poem, to console him in his hours of affliction (v. 9, 10), both of which he is compelled, however unwillingly, to deny him (v. 31, 32); the books, because he is living at Verona and has only a small case (*capsula*) with him; the poem, because his brother's death weighs too heavy on his mind to admit of his devoting himself to such a task.

---

* I have a strong impression that Coelius, not Allius, is the person to whom this poem is addressed. Cf. v. 51-56 with Carm. c. v. 5-7.

After these statements, it is impossible to conceive that Catullus, *on the spot*, wrote to him a long poem.

2*d*. The second poem contradicts the first—
v. 1-8, and 155, 156;
v. 25, 26, and 159, 160.

3*d*. Catullus would be made to repeat himself, which he does nowhere else in the same poem—
v. 20-24, and 92-96.

4*th*. One poem clearly ends at line 40, while another as clearly begins at line 41.

CARM. LXVIII.ᵃ v. 13.

——qucis merser fortunae fluctibus ipse.

Cf. Aesch. Prom. Vinct. v. 746—
Δυσχείμερόν γε πέλαγος ἀτηρᾶς δύης.

V. 29.   Frigida deserto tepefecit membra cubili.

Cf. Tibull. i. 8, 27-30—

> Nec tu difficilis puero tamen esse memento,
>   Persequitur poenis tristia facta Venus,
> Munera nec poscas : det munera canus amator,
>   Ut foveas molli frigida membra sinu.

> Then be not to thy swain unkind and sour,
>   For Venus vengeance takes on shameful slights,
> Nor sue for gifts—the hoary lover's dower—
>   To make thee thaw his frozen limbs o' nights.

CARM. LXVIII.ᵇ v. 49-50.

> Nec tenuem texens sublimis aranea telam,
>   In deserto, Alli, nomine opus faciat.

Cf. Propert. iv. 5, 31-34 (iii. 6, 31-34)—

> Si non vana canunt mea somnia, Lygdame, testor,
>   Poena erit ante meos sera, sed ampla, pedes;
> Putris et in vacuo texetur aranea lecto :
>   Noctibus illorum dormiet ipsa Venus.

> If but my dreams bode truth, then vengeance dread,
> Though late, shall at my feet be amply paid,
> The flimsy cobweb line their vacant bed,
> And love sleep all night long though fondly pray'd.

V. 53.
>> Cum tantum arderem, quantum Trinacria rupes.

Cf. Byron—
> But mine was like the lava flood
> That boils in Aetna's breast of flame.

And Ovid, Rem. Amor. 491-494—
> Quamvis infelix media torreberis Aetna,
> Frigidior glacie fac videare tuae:
> Et sanum simula, ne, siquid forte dolebis,
> Sentiat, et ride, cum tibi flendus eris.

> Though Aetna's flames should scorch thy love-sick heart,
> The semblance of an icy coldness keep;
> Seem heart-whole, lest she know thy bosom's smart,
> And smile although thou feel'st inclined to weep.

V. 62.
>> Cum gravis exustos aestus hiulcat agros.

Cf. Tibull. i. 7, 17, 21, 22—
> Quid referam ————
> Qualis et, arentes cum findit Sirius agros,
> Fertilis aestiva Nilus abundet aqua?

> Why tell ————
> How fertile Nile with summer floods abounds
> When scorching Sirius cracks the heat-baked grounds?

V. 70, 71.
>> Quo mea se molli candida Diva pede
>> Intulit.

Cf. Propert. iii. 3, 21-24, (ii. 12, 21-24)—
> Quam si perdideris, quis erit qui talia cantet?
> (Haec mea Musa levis gloria magna tua est,)

> Qui caput et digitos et lumina nigra puellae
> Et canat *ut soleant molliter ire pedes?*

> Quench it (umbra mea), from whom will then such songs
>   arise?
> (My Muse, though lowly, is thy glory great),
> Who then will sing thy head and jet-black eyes,
> Thy lovely fingers, *and thy mincing gait?*

V. 71, 72.

> ——— et trito fulgentem in limine plantam
> Innixa, arguta constitit in solea.

Cf. Propert. iii. 27, 39-42, (ii. 29, 39-42)—

> Dixit, et opposita propellens savia dextra
> *Prosilit in laxa nixa pedem solea.*
> Sic ego tam sancti custode recludor amoris:
> Ex illo felix nox mihi nulla fuit.

> She spoke: with her right hand my kiss opposed,
> *Then in loose sandal darted from my sight.*
> Thus prying care love's hallow'd temple closed:
> Since then I have not known one happy night.

V. 83.

> Noctibus in longis avidum saturasset amorem.

Cf. Ovid. Heroid. xiii. 103-106, (Laodamia scribit)—

> Sive latet Phoebus, seu terris altior exstat,
>   Tu mihi luce dolor, tu mihi nocte venis:
> Nocte tamen quam luce magis; nox grata puellis,
>   Quarum suppositus colla lacertus habet.

> Then whether reigns the day or reigns the night,
>   Thou art my thought by night, my thought by day—
> Night more than day—night is the girl's delight,
>   Who on a lover's arm her neck can lay.

ILLUSTRATIVE NOTES. 281

V. 109-116.   Quale——foret.

Cf. Tibull. iii. 4, 65-68—

> Saevus Amor docuit validos tentare labores,
> Saevus Amor docuit verbera saeva pati.
> Me quondam Admeti niveas pavisse juvencas
> Non est in vanum fabula ficta jocum.

> His votaries Love hath taught by stern behest
> Hard toils to bear, beneath the lash to bleed,
> 'Tis no vain fable framed for idle jest
> That I Admetus' snow-white flocks did feed.

V. 115, 116.

> Pluribus ut coeli tereretur janua Divis
> Hebe nec longa virginitate foret.

Cf. Hom. Odyss. xi. 602, 603—

> ―――― αὐτὸς δὲ μετ' ἀθανάτοισι θεοῖσιν
> Τέρπεται ἐν θαλίῃς καὶ ἔχει καλλίσφυρον Ἥβην.

> He banquets now the immortal gods beside,
> With beauteous-ankled Hebe for his bride.

V. 125-128.   Nec ―――― mulier.

Cf. Propert. iii. 7, 27-30, (ii. 15, 27-30)—

> Exemplo junctae tibi sint in amore columbae,
> Masculus et totum femina conjugium.
> Errat, qui finem vesani quaerit amoris :
> Verus amor nullum novit habere modum.

> The faithful doves be pattern of our joy,
> That each with each in fond affection vie;
> He errs who would love's frenzied flame destroy;
> True love can never know satiety.

Mart. xi. 104, 9—

> Basia me capiunt blandas imitata columbas.

And again, Epigr. xii. 65, 7-9—

>   Amplexa collum, basioque tam longo
>   Blandita, quam sunt nuptiae columbarum,
>   Rogare coepit Phyllis amphoram vini.

>   She clasps my neck, her lips to mine she presses,
>   Long as when mating dove fond dove caresses,
>   " What asks my Phyllis, Phyllis the divine ? "
>   " Nothing, love, nothing but a jar of wine."

V. 133, 134.

>   ——— Cupido
>   Fulgebat crocina candidus in tunica.

So Quintus Calaber v. 71.

>   Κύπρις ἐϋστέφανος, τὴν δ'ἵμερος ἀμφεποτᾶτο.

V. 145, 146.

>   Sed furtiva dedit mira munuscula nocte,
>   Ipsius ex ipso demta viri gremio.

Cf. Burns—

>   O May, thy morn was ne'er sae sweet,
>   As the mirk night o' December;
>   For sparkling was the rosy wine,
>   And private was the chamber,
>   And dear was she I darena name,
>   But I will aye remember.

V. 147, 148.

>   Quare illud satis est, si nobis is datur unus,
>   *Quem lapide illa diem candidiore notat.*

Cf. Catull. cvii. 6, and Mart. Epigr. xii. 34—

>   Triginta mihi quatuorque messes
>   Tecum, si memini, fuere, Juli :
>   Quarum dulcia mixta sunt amaris ;
>   Sed jucunda tamen fuere plura.

> *Et si calculus omnis huc et illuc*
> *Diversus bicolorque digeratur :*
> *Vincet candida turba nigriorem.*
> Si vitare velis acerba quaedam,
> Et tristes animi cavere morsus,
> Nulli te facias nimis sodalem.
> Gaudebis minus, et minus dolebis.

> Julius we 've now together spent
>   Some four and thirty years ;
> We 've found life's sweets with bitters blent,
>   But aye more smiles than tears.
>
> *Could we life's diverse stones now view,*
>   *Strewn twin-hued here and there,*
> *And part them : those of darker hue*
>   *Would not outsum the fair.*
>
> If thou some bitter things wouldst shun
>   In life's uneven course,
> And have thy days more smoothly run,
>   Ungall'd by fell remorse ;
>
> Though many friends should round thee press,
>   Take none too close to thee,
> And if thy joys should be the less,
>   Less, too, thy griefs will be.

V. 155.
         Sitis felices et tu simul et tua vita.

A common formula, *vide* Tibull. iii. 6, 27-30—

> Quid precor ah demens ? venti temeraria vota,
>   Aeriae et nubes diripienda ferant.
> Quamvis nulla mei superest tibi cura, Neaera,
>   Sis felix, et sint candida fata tua.

> No—let my rash and frantic wishes be
>   Dispersed by winds and clouds athwart the air :
> Neaera, though thou ne'er shouldst think of me,
>   Mayst thou be blest, and may thy fate be fair.

POEM LXIX.

V. 1. Noli admirari, quare tibi femina nulla,
Rufe, velit *tenerum supposuisse femur.*

Cf. Tibull. i. 8, 23–26—

> Quid queror heu misero carmen nocuisse, quid herbas?
> Forma nihil magicis utitur auxiliis:
> Sed corpus tetigisse nocet, sed longa dedisse
> Oscula, sed *femori conseruisse femur.*

> Why blame I spell or herb? in that or this
> Beauty no secret, magic aid doth find,
> 'Tis in the claspèd hand, the long, long kiss,
> *And form with form all lovingly entwined.*

V. 3, 4.

> Non ullam rarae labefactes munere vestis
> Aut pelluciduli deliciis lapidis.

Cf. Tibull. ii. 3, 51–54—

> Ut mea luxuria Nemesis fluat utque per urbem
> Incedat donis conspicienda meis.
> Illa gerat vestes tenues, quas femina Coa
> Texuit, auratas' disposuitque vias.

> Then swim in wealth and gifts, my love; let none
> Walk through the streets more gorgeous to behold;
> Wear silken robes by Coan maiden spun,
> And curiously inwrought with thread of gold.

And ii. 4, 27–30, where the same poet, in quite a different humour, sings of the Coan robe—

> O pereat, quicunque legit viridesque smaragdos
> Et niveam Tyrio murice tingit ovem,
> Hic dat avaritiae causas et Coa puellis,
> Vestis et e rubro lucida concha mari.

>   Perish the man who gathers emeralds green,
>   And dyes the snowy wool with Tyrian shell,
>   These, Coan robes, and Red Sea pearls, I ween,
>   Have fill'd with avarice many an artless belle.

V. 6.   Valle *sub alarum trux habitare caper.*

Cf. Ovid. Art. Am. i. 522—

>   Nec laedat naris *virque paterque gregis.*

And Art. Am. iii. 193—

>   Quam paene admonui, ne *trux caper iret in alas.*

POEM LXX.

V. 1, 2.
Cf. Catull. lxxii. 1, 2.

V. 3, 4.

>   Dicit: sed mulier cupido quod dicit amanti,
>   In vento, et rapida scribere oportet aqua.

Cf. Tibull. i. 4, 21-24—

>   Nec jurare time: Veneris perjuria venti
>   Irrita per terras et freta summa ferunt.
>   Gratia magna Jovi: vetuit pater ipse valere,
>   Jurasset cupide quicquid ineptus amor.

>   Fear not to swear: by winds athwart the air
>   Are love's false vows o'er earth and ocean borne;
>   Great thanks to Jove: who hath annull'd whate'er
>   Incautious love too eagerly hath sworn.

And iii. 6, 47-50—

>   Etsi perque suos fallax juravit ocellos
>   Junonemque suam perque suam Venerem,
>   Nulla fides inerit: perjuria ridet amantum
>   Jupiter et ventos irrita ferre jubet.

> Though the deceitful maiden by her eyes
> And by her Venus and her Juno swear,
> Trust not: Jove smiles at lovers' perjuries,
> And bids the breezes scatter them in air.

Cf. with v. 4. Epigr. Meleagr. civ. 5 (Edit. Mans.)—

Νῦν δ' ὁ μὲν ὅρκιά φησιν ἐν ὕδατι κεῖνα φέρεσθαι.

POEM LXXIII.

V. 3.

Omnia sunt ingrata: nihil fecisse benigne est.

Cf. Hom. Odyss. iv. 695—

———οὐδέ τις ἔστι χάρις μετόπισθ' εὐεργέων.

POEM LXXXIII.

Cf. Catull. xcii.

POEM LXXXV.

Odi et amo. Quare id faciam, fortasse requiris.
Nescio: sed fieri sentio, et excrucior.

Cf. Terent. Eunuch. 70–73.

> ———O indignum facinus! nunc ego
> Et illam scelestam esse, et me miserum sentio;
> Et taedet; et amore ardeo; et prudens, sciens,
> Vivus vidensque pereo; nec, quid agam, scio.

> Oh, foul indignity! at last I see
> Her faithlessness, and feel my misery,
> I loathe and burn, know, see, and feel this, too,
> That I'm undone: I know not what to do.

Poem LXXXVI.

V. 5, 6.   Lesbia ——— Veneres.

Cf. Burns—
>She, the fair sun of all her sex,
>Has blest my glorious day.

Poem XCV.

V. 8.   Et laxas scombris saepe dabunt tunicas.

Cf. Mart. Epigr. iv. 87, 8—
>Nec scombris tunicas dabis molestas.

Poem XCVI.

Si quidquam, &c.

Vide Propert. iii. 32, 87-94 (ii. 34, 87-94)—
>Haec quoque lascivi cantarunt scripta Catulli,
>   Lesbia quis ipsa notior est Helena.
>Haec etiam docti confessa est pagina Calvi,
>   Cum caneret miserae funera Quintiliae.
>Et modo formosa quam multa Lycoride Gallus
>   Mortuus inferna vulnera lavit aqua!
>Cynthia quin etiam versu laudata Properti,
>   Hos inter si me ponere Fama volet.

>This was the theme of warm Catullus' lays,
>   That made his Lesbia's more than Helen's fame,
>Thus learned Calvus told Quintilia's praise,
>   Bewailed her death, and sung her honour'd name.

> How many wounds from fair Lycoris' scorn
> Poor Gallus now has wash'd in Lethe's stream !
> But Cynthia, too, will live to times unborn,
> If fame will but indulge her poet's dream.

POEM CI.

V. 10.

> Atque in perpetuum, frater, ave atque vale.

Cf. Virg. Aen. xi. 97, 98—

> ——Salve aeternum mihi, maxime Palla,
> Aeternumque vale !

> > Hail ! noblest Pallas, hail for evermore !
> > For evermore farewell !

And Stat. Silv. iii. 3, 208, 209—

> Salve supremum, senior mitissime patrum
> Supremumque vale.

POEM CVII.

V. 3.

> Quare hoc est gratum, nobis quoque carius auro.

Cf. Tibull. i. 8, 31-34—

> Carior est auro juvenis, cui levia fulgent
>   Ora nec amplexus aspera barba terit.
> Huic tu candentes humero suppone lacertos,
>   Et regum magnae despiciantur opes.

> Dearer than gold the youth with smooth blithe face,
>   And no rough beard love's fond embrace to mar;
> Thine ivory arm beneath his shoulder place,
>   And scorn the wealth of kings—thou 'rt richer far.

With this poem, *passim*, compare Tibull. iii. 3, 23-38—

>Sit mihi paupertas tecum jucunda, Neaera :
> At sine te regum munera nulla volo.
>O niveam, quae te poterit mihi reddere, lucem !
> O mihi felicem terque quaterque diem !
>At si, pro dulci reditu quaecunque voventur,
> Audiat aversa non meus aure deus,
>Nec me regna juvant nec Lydius aurifer amnis
> Nec quas terrarum sustinet orbis opes.
>Haec alii cupiant, liceat mihi paupere cultu
> Securo cara conjuge posse frui.
>Adsis et timidis faveas, Saturnia, votis,
> Et faveas concha, Cypria, vecta tua.
>Aut, si fata negant reditum tristesque sorores,
> Stamina quae ducunt quaeque futura neunt,
>Me vocet in vastos amnes nigramque paludem
> Dives in ignava luridus Orcus aqua.

>With thee, Neaera, want has wealth of charms ;
> The gifts of kings I scorn, deprived of thee ;
>Bright light that will restore thee to my arms !
> Oh thrice and four times happy day to me !

>Should Love, with favouring smile, my care behold,
> And hear my vows breathed for thy sweet return,
>Then Lydia's river, rolling sands of gold,
> Realms, and the wealth of worlds, I'll proudly spurn.

>Let others covet these : on humble fare
> Let me with thee, mine own, serenely dwell ;
>Come, Juno, smile on this my timid prayer,
> Smile, Cyprian goddess, wafted on thy shell.

>But if the Fates deny the boon I crave,
> Grim Three who draw and spin the threads of doom,
>Hell ! call me to thy lurid, sluggish wave,
> Thy gulfy streams, and marsh of ebon gloom.

And Hor. Od. iii. 9—

>*Horace.* While I was all in all to thee,
> Nor any swain preferr'd to me,

    Round your fair neck his arms dared fling,
      I scorn'd even Persia's king.

Lydia. While for no other fair you burn'd,
    Nor Chloe look'd on Lydia spurn'd,
    An honour'd head I then could rear,
      For Ilia more than peer.

Horace. Now Chloe thrills me with desire,
    A lady skill'd on lute or lyre,
    For whom the darts of death I'll prove,
      If heaven will spare my love.

Lydia. I and my Thurian Caläis
    Together live in mutual bliss,
    For whom I'll die and die again,
      If heaven will spare my swain.

Horace. Should Venus once again provoke
    Us both to try love's brazen yoke,
    And fair-hair'd Chloe leave my home,
      Oh, say, would Lydia come?

Lydia. Though fairer than the sun he shone,
    Thou light as down by breezes blown,
    And fretful as the raging sea,
      I'd live, I'd die with thee.

POEM CX.

Cf. Priap. ii. (Ovidii) "Priapus."

  Obscure poteram tibi dicere, da mihi, quod tu
    Des licet assidue, nil tamen inde perit.
  Da mihi, quod cupies frustra dare forsitan olim,
    Dum tenet obsessas invida barba genas;
  Quodque Jovi dederat, qui, raptus ab alite sacra,
    Miscet amatori pocula grata suo;

Quod virgo prima cupido dat nocte marito,
   Dum timet alterius vulnus inepta loci.
Simplicius multo est, da paedicare, Latine
   Dicere; quid faciam? Crassa Minerva mea est.

Love, a kiss I did covertly ask;
   And, believe me, such tokens I prize;
Though you ply evermore the sweet task,
   Oh remember the charm never dies.

Come, then, grant me the favour I seek,
   Or your coyness you yet may regret,
When the wrinkle has furrow'd your cheek,
   And the sun of your beauty is set.

When the all-sacred eagle pick'd up
   And presented young Gan to King Jove,
First the little chap mix'd him a cup,
   And then shower'd on him kisses of love.

On the night when a maiden is wed,
   And her fond lover calls her his own,
Although many a thought fills her head,
   Wont she give him a kiss when alone?

Come, then, come to my arms, darling true!
   In plain language, come, kiss me at once:
Oh consent, love, or what shall I do?
   He who misses a chance is a dunce.

POEM CXIII.

V. 2.   Mucillam (Mucilla?).

Ballantyne & Company, Printers, Edinburgh.

www.ingramcontent.com/pod-product-compliance
Lightning Source LLC
Chambersburg PA
CBHW022117230426
43672CB00008B/1410